THE JOY OF
SLIMMING

by
Christopher Hills, Ph.D., D.Sc.

Microalgae International Sales Corporation
Boulder Creek, CA 95006

Dr. Hills has researched nutrition and pioneered the production of microalgae as a new technology for feeding the world since 1960. He is not a medical doctor. If you are having health problems of any kind, you should check with your physician before beginning any kind of diet or exercise program.

Library of Congress Cataloging in Publication Data

Hills, Christopher B.
    The joy of slimming.

    1. Reducing diets.   2. Reducing—Psychological
aspects.   3. Spirulina—Therapeutic use.   4. Food,
Natural.   I. Title.
RM222.2.H48   1982   613.2'5   82–14452
ISBN 0–916438–48–1 (pbk.)

TABLE
OF CONTENTS

ACKNOWLEDGEMENTS

Many versions of this plan were tried by my students in its preliminary form. The first effort was a fat book, full of scientific facts about fat metabolism, nutrition information and things to do. Several of my students helped me to see that I had not given much time to making the book interesting. I wish to thank them for their efforts to make the Plan easy and fun.

I particularly wish to thank Dr. Ann Ray for taking my manuscript and editing it down from a thick book and making it a more palatable diet plan. I also must thank those many students, distributors and friends who tried and tested Spirulina and the diet products experimentally before putting the Plan into print.

I wish to thank all of you who have spontaneously written me over the last few years telling me of your success with weight loss through my rejuvenation books. Even if I cannot acknowledge your efforts in public, please do write me and share your success. You are the real heroes who persevere and conquer your appetites. I'd love to see the before and after pictures to prove what you did.

Remember, there is a double motive in the Slimming Plan. As you eat Spirulina and become slim, you are helping someone else less fortunate to get fatter, because all available profits have been dedicated by me to scientifically feeding a hungry world. Thank you for helping.

PART I

DR. HILLS SLIMMING PLAN

A PERSONAL MESSAGE FROM DR. HILLS

When I was about thirty years old I decided to change my life and travel the world to find out if there were any wise men who had discovered the secret of eternal youth. I travelled to all those places in Afghanistan on the border of Russia where old people lived well over a hundred years. I was the thirtieth person from the West to visit Hunza and learn the so-called secrets of their healthy life. I travelled wherever I heard there was some special skill or gift of healing. It was a long trip and I finished up knowing a lot of people all over the planet. I kept up with them for years until I could no longer keep 1,700 names in my memory. So for several years I wrote hundreds of letters every week until one day I realized none of this correspondence was really of any importance unless it changed me or changed the world in some vital way. In other words, I got tired of words, papers, books, theories and concepts and longed for something real to happen. So one day I burnt all my files and saw the work of years and thousands of days of effort all disappear in smoke. It was then I decided that unless a person can actually manifest more than words, books, papers, etc. in life, he or she is going to die disappointed, disillusioned and dispirited.

But what can an ordinary person achieve that will change life into something thrilling and dynamic? I decided the first thing was to get mastery over myself—my appetites, my attachments to people, money, food, power, fame, and inaccurate knowledge that defeat our lives over and over again. Embarking on this task was not easy but I discovered everything became easy, once you knew how to do something well. In doing something well, I found it was easier if I could find someone who had already spent a lot of time researching and thinking things through. In short, starting where other people had left off became my philosophy. First find out everything other people know, then find out what they don't know! When you narrow down to what they don't know, you begin to experiment in real ways to get first-hand knowledge. That is "self-mastery", to get first-hand knowledge so that you are never dependent on some other authority.

The "philosophy of phat" has this one aim, because you can then experiment with your own body. Your body is a fantastic chemical laboratory in which you are the chemist and the researcher into the secrets of life. I found there is no need to travel the world, go searching in the desert for messiahs or listening to so-called experts. Listen to everyone, most of all to yourself, and do your own research in the laboratory of your own body and you will be amazed that you can actually free yourself from your dependency on others, on governments, or on seeking answers outside your own consciousness.

If you only knew how powerful your consciousness is, you would know immediately why you are fat or thin or depressed or suffering from ill health. But to know the nature of your consciousness, the power of your own hang-ups and the strengths and weaknesses of your own ego is not something a teacher can do for you. It is not something a guru or expert or friend can help you with, except to give advice. Eventually you must do the work on yourself because you and no one else can really clean up the mess in your own mind. Physical mess can easily be cleaned up, but psychological mess is just as difficult for a President of the United States, with all the power of the government behind him, as it is for you or me.

The "philosophy of phat" is my attempt to give you in the fewest words possible, the essence of how to do it. At first I wrote a whole thick book of facts, but I figured you would soon get bored with all that technical research when all you wanted to do was get thin. So the fat in this book was ruthlessly cut down to a thin book which had just the answers you need and no more. But you can thank your lucky stars that you don't just have a diet book in your hands with a lot of words telling you what to do. What you've got is a whole group of real weapons and research tools to take into the battle of the bulge. Spirulina is a Godsend in this battle which makes it so easy. Also the other products like the galacto-mannans in Fiber-Lean enable you to start off where most other diet plans leave off.

Remember, the essence of this "philosophy of phat" is not just to control your appetite for food but to get a handle on your appetite for everything; in short, "self-mastery". You are welcome to get my two thick fat books (1000 pages each) written for researchers on self-mastery, which both have more to do with the nature of the human mind and soul. But first it is important to get a disciplined body, an efficient vehicle for the spirit to function in, a healthy vessel for a healthy mind. Remember, it is much easier to put something in your mouth and stomach than to put something into your mind. So begin with the Spirulina and then go on and on discovering your power over your own life. Don't stop just when you get thin, because you want to stay thin and find the secret of eternal youth. Every day I feel like a newborn baby and I am a kid at heart who will never get discouraged at the negative way the grown-ups get or the way the world gets screwed up. When my body dies, it will be a youthful one. I hope you too can learn to be young at heart, spontaneous and radiant.*

---

*Send me a picture of you before you start your diet and then send me another picture showing what you as a whole person have achieved in a few months' time. We would like to follow your success. So many thousands of people have been changed and become sparkling and radiant on my products that I want to see you keeping up your rejuvenation.

DIETING FOR THE WHOLE PERSON

Wherever you are, whoever you are, do not be afraid to try something new. Some of you have had a weight problem for years, or maybe all your life. But you do not have to have it anymore. The "Dr. Hills Slimming Plan" is a completely new and revolutionary way to lose weight. You will see for yourself how quickly new confidence comes in and old doubts go out, once you decide to take into your own hands the shaping of your own consciousness. Once you do that, the shaping of your physical body is no longer difficult.

Mrs. Hills and I have spent the last thirty-two years in the study of human awareness and we have learned one thing—that your consciousness is the most powerful energy in the universe. It can turn you into any kind of person you want to be. And this is the real purpose of my Slimming Plan. Getting slim is only the by-product. But there is one thing you must have in order to make it work for you, and that one thing is receptivity. By now you have probably tried many diets and you've counted calories and eaten raw vegetables and all the rest, so you may be feeling, "None of that stuff works". In fact, you may be feeling that nothing in the world could possibly help you be who you really want to be. So you are going to have to put some real energy into opening your mind to the fact that help is coming to you now in a form that may not seem new but which may evoke in you the power to completely transform your life.

My Slimming Plan is a plan you can live with happily, eating what you like on certain days while losing weight and at the same time keeping your body fit with excellent nutrition. On free days you will eat and drink what you like in whatever quantity and not feel guilty on three days of every week. Free days make the difference between staying on the diet and giving it up! Most people give up diets because they feel deprived or because they get bored with buying special foods or counting calories. Free days are your reward days and you can eat on special days or holidays without being a traitor to your diet just by switching your free days with the days you eat the special Dr. Hills' diet products. Free days are balanced by "shape up" days.

Whatever the cause of your weight problem, this Slimming Plan can help you change it. I know this because I have worked with all kinds of people with all kinds of hurdles to overcome. They all have one thing in common—they just need to see what will set them free. Here in Boulder Creek we have people who have changed even the shape of their *faces* by first changing their consciousness. And many have changed their bodies. My secretary Pamela Osborn, who has been with me for seven years, has changed both body and mind, as she will tell you herself:

I had been on a near continual diet since I turned age 14 and steered away from those salami and potato chip sandwiches I used to eat in my school lunches. I wanted to be attractive like all the models in the magazines but it was one constant struggle as I ballooned and then starved myself and thinned a bit and then ballooned, and back and forth it went. I used to get so starved and weak from my diets that I would become ravenous and gorge myself or go for the sugar as I felt so tired and draggy. Eventually I came to run a couple of miles each day just to be able to maintain my size at "chubby". I no longer have a fat personality, because Dr. Hills, my friend and mentor, has at last got me to see that the root of the whole problem is in my state of consciousness, not in my body. He showed me where I felt empty inside and showed me how to fill that emptiness with the fulfillment of caring regard for myself and for others.

Here is Pam Osborn before she changed her consciousness and after. When the first picture was taken, Pam was a complete hedonist and lived for pleasure—boyfriends, good food, wine, scuba diving, and entertainment. The second picture, taken in July 1982, shows a Pam that is master of her appetites and has chosen to put her abundant energy into serving her fellowman through the Light Force Company. As her own father recently said to Dr. Hills, "I believe in what you are doing, because I can see the beautiful change in my daughter. She's a completely different person".

In my own life, I have had to contend with several weaknesses or sometimes just the opposite—an excess of strength. The worst one was pride. I had so much pride in what I already knew, that I couldn't hear the voice of Wisdom if it shouted in my ear. At one time I read so many books that my forehead grew about two inches taller than it is now. I thought, "My head looks funny. I can't remember it being this tall before." *Once I realized what was causing it*, I stopped filling my head with worthless knowledge and it went back down to its normal size. Sounds like science fiction, doesn't it? I wish I had a picture to show you. It would be a picture of a vain human being who knew all there was to know except the most important thing. There is a reason why people are called "egg heads".

Now if I shrunk my head by giving up a little pride, surely you can shrink your body! You know I get a lot of letters from people who have a lot of pride and judge me without even reading my work or knowing my true purpose, and they think they have the only answer. I won't preach to you like that because I know that a fat body is no different from my problem of a fat head. Stubbornness is human. If I tell you to lay off the cookies, you will go and eat one. If I condemn junk foods, you will want what is forbidden. So I say to you, eat what you like but remember feast days are free days and on the other days you keep your promise to my rule of diet for "shape up" days.

This day marks for you the beginning of a new relationship with your body and its totally unique metabolic system. Hour by hour, day by day, you will learn what works for you. Concentrate on the positive goal of health and fitness, not on the negative goal of losing weight. Dr. Hills Slimming Plan is not only a plan for reclaiming the body but for completely restructuring the inner world of thoughts. Therefore, *it is the last diet you will ever have to begin*. Do not be afraid to indulge in optimism, for you are standing on the threshold of a whole new world unfolding to your view. Throw fatalism out of the window. You do not have to be any longer whatever you have been up to now. I can eat ice cream sundaes or anything on the menu and so can you and still stay on your diet.

Here's How

There are many approaches to dieting. Some systems approach the problem chemically and calculate exactly what food elements will help you burn off fat. Other systems depend on will power but ignore the pain of hunger which will power cannot cope with. So you end up feeling you have failed and perhaps despising yourself for it when in fact it was impossible from the outset. Still other systems deal with attitudes and feelings, but they do not go deep enough to make more than a superficial change in your consciousness. The Dr. Hills Slimming Plan is unique in that it offers just one or two simple techniques which can help you become the person you want to be. The first step is to get to know yourself.

All people are different. They do their best to hide it, but if they really expressed their real essence, each one is different. It is a pity that we go through life trying to re-make ourselves in our sister's or our brother's image or trying to live up to our parents' expectations. If we could find out who we are deeper down, in the part of us we seldom show to anyone, we would also know how our own unique body system works and what makes it feel best. Some of us eat, even when we are not really hungry, because our problem is not physical hunger but psychological hunger. And in the same way, we try to be like everyone else because we have a need to belong, and yet we may have an even deeper hunger that we don't even know about—a hunger to be our own unique Self. Some are religious for the same reason, but most people don't realize that the sages told us how to eat. They told us not to fill the stomach but to stop at three-quarters full. "Eat what you like and stop" may sound very difficult for some people. I will show you how to be different, how to become your true shapely self.

Even in the matter of weight, we are conformists and do not take into account our life situations which may require of us quite different body weights. You may think, "The girl I love likes tall wiry fellows, whereas I am stocky and muscular. What I need is to look like them. Then I will win her love." Do you really want to base the new you on the off chance of pleasing someone else, be it mother, father, friend or sweetheart? We are talking about discovering who you really are, which is the best thing you can ever wish to be.

How do you find out who you really are? This is easier than it seems because you already know who you are, down under the layers of false portraits that have been heaped upon you by yourself and by others since the day you were born. Occasionally you might get a strong feeling of something you really care about or something you really want to do or say. You deny the feeling because it doesn't fit what you think you are supposed to be. But these feelings are coming from your real nature.

In the old myths of the world, whether Greek or Roman or Egyptian or those of our own American Indians, one theme runs through almost every story. At some point the hero is given a charm or an amulet by some wise old man or woman, and without this little extra boost, he would not have the strength to do battle with the powerful forces he must master, which are usually none other than the fears, doubts and negative energies and projections of his own mind, represented in symbolic form as dragons and demons. If I were to give you an amulet for the little extra strength you will need to master whatever is causing you to gain weight, I would give you a key. And with this key you would be able to unlock the secret of your own particular destiny, for I believe that each soul, no matter how seemingly ordinary, has a destiny, and the key to it is a little movie camera, hidden inside the mind, which records every thought, every word and every action of your life. Watch that movie and you will see something you have not seen before. If you watch your thoughts very closely you will find yourself feeling things you didn't know you felt. You may find that you love someone you thought you hated. Or you may find that your mind makes up fantasies or makes up elaborate dialogues between you and other people. Maybe you even feel superior or better than they! Unless you make a conscious effort to see these thoughts and feelings, you won't even be aware that they are there, because all of us have not only a conscious mind but also an unconscious mind.

What's Down There?

Thanks to Sigmund Freud, C.G. Jung, and other pioneers of psychology, most of us know that we have an unconscious mind, but we are not exactly sure what it is, and it seems not to matter much, so we ignore it and go on about our lives. But the unconscious mind is not a concept or a theory. It is as much a part of us as are our legs and feet and hands and arms! If consciously we are saying, "I'm slim and beautiful" but unconsciously we are saying, "I'm fat and ugly," we will soon be fat and ugly if we are not so already, because the unconscious mind has enormous power to manifest in our lives, whether we give our conscious permission or not. In fact, an unconscious feeling or attitude has much more power than a conscious one, simply because it is unseen and unknown. It sneaks up on us, so to speak. We feel *compelled* to do or say something, even if it is completely irrational.

How do things get into the unconscious? When we are children, perhaps our mother often remarks, "If you keep that up, you're going to be fat like your father." Our memory records this message again and again, "You're going to be fat." But we are busy climbing trees and running about and we are not consciously thinking about that little tape recorder in our brain. Ten or twenty years later, that phrase may manifest as a desire to eat. It is no use pointing the finger of blame at mother or teacher or whatever put those thoughts into our minds, because these are an inevitable part of life, and every human being grows up with an unconscious mind. Only a very few people realize that by becoming conscious of the thoughts and feelings which have formerly been unconscious, we can take away their power once and for all. To do this, you have to start watching your mind, yet without becoming self-obsessed and selfish. Watch especially the thoughts that you censor: "I wish he were dead. Oh no, I don't really mean that. I take it back." Start being more real with yourself. Own up to your feelings, including the ones that are not so nice. At first you may feel like you are a terrible person, but really you are no more terrible than anyone else. We all have good and bad qualities. Some of us face ourselves and start to work on the bad. Others are afraid to face what they are and they shove all the bad, or what *seems* to be bad, into unconsciousness. But in fact some of the seeming bad may be our best qualities in disguise, and we will discover this once we begin to be honest with ourselves and risk bringing them to light. People tend to think of the unconscious mind as a storehouse full of monsters and unwanted feelings. Actually it is also the place where positive qualities are stored and the place where your incredible potential lies waiting to be summoned up by your consciousness.

Once you begin to watch the signals from your own consciousness which tell you which choices are right for you and which are not, you will also begin to notice that your craving for food is not just plain ordinary craving; it is very specific. Many people eat because they have some need which they are unable to fill, so they fill their stomachs instead. It may be a need for recognition or acceptance. It may be a need to be important and to have their opinions "carry weight". In some, it is the need to be loved. In others it is the need to *make* love. Many human needs are really a need to experience our *own* love flowing out to others. It *feels* like a desire to *get* love, but really it is a desire to give. And the only way to get love or anything else is to give it. So if we wait around hoping that love and respect and appreciation will find us, we may wait a whole lifetime, and while we wait, we eat.

Why Do You Eat Sweets?

Is your craving for a sweetheart moving your arm toward a cookie? Or is it a desire to be free that makes you settle for a bit of forbidden fruit? Would you like to tell your mother or your father or your boss to go to blazes but you put it off? What do you do instead? You put your hand in the candy jar!

No one but you knows why you eat too many sweets. And no one but you can make a new habit to replace the old one. Better yet, go on and tell them to go to blazes or whatever it is that you need to do. If you do not know how to find out the cause, try asking yourself these questions:

1. What am I feeling just before I eat the cookie or the candy or the cake?
2. What am I feeling just afterward?
3. Are there certain times when I don't seem to need a sweet?
4. When do I most crave it?
5. Is there any person who seems to make me want a sweet or want to eat junk food?
6. Is there anyone who makes me forget all about it?

LOVE IS THE SWEETEST THING THERE IS!!!

THE JOY OF BEING SLENDER

Photography by John Hills and John Motelewski, Nagamine Camera of Lahaina, Maui. Courtesy of the Kapalua Bay Hotel.

THE FUN OF EATING

Once you understand the basic principle of what makes you gain weight, then Dr. Hills Slimming Plan is easy. Your cells crave nourishment because your emotions crave nourishment, and you eat compulsively because you really need something to fill up the big lonely hole inside. So you eat and eat to compensate for what you're not getting in other areas of life because you feel empty inside. When you realize this you also realize that you are putting your hands inside the fridge door or tearing open another bag of pretzels, cookies or sweets because you don't feel full and filled (fulfilled!).

So the magic words that you say to yourself over and over, when you're gaining weight and can't stop eating, are not that you have to deny yourself or go on a quick fast or pay through the nose to go to a weight loss club. The magic words are simple and you say them over and over—
I am feeling empty
because I am not
FULL FILLED

So you say the word fulfilled, fulfilled, fulfilled over and over until you say to yourself, "What will make me fulfilled?" Then you sit down and make a check list of what will make you fulfilled:
Better job
More money
More love
Proper relationship with mate
Understanding from someone dear
Religious truth
Spiritual purpose
Success in business
Emotional security
Meaningful activity
Better health
Work on the first desire or goal on the list. If you want a better

job, scan all the ads, get a good resumé typed out, smarten yourself up for interviews and go after the job you want most. Put energy into the search, get excited at the prospect of a new and challenging job. Remember, the fulfillment of your goals is in *your* hands. If *you* don't act, no one else is going to hand you fulfillment on a plate! Maybe you want to deal with them all. But it is best if you cover just one at a time in the right order of importance for you. When you get the first goal mastered, you move onto another. In other words, priority of your goal is important. DON'T TRY TO MASTER EVERYTHING AT ONCE. If you tackle everything you will do nothing, because you will then rationalize that it is too difficult, and once you do that rationalizing, you're back with your fingers into the fridge and you go out and eat six donuts to give yourself a treat, just to make yourself feel better. Your cells will crave because of what you are missing. That's the basic premise of Dr. Hills Slimming Plan.

So how do you compensate in other areas? You can't suck your thumb instead of a sweetie and get satisfaction. Dr. Hills Slimming Plan claims that if you can master this one word— FULL FILLED—you will feel *filled full* and won't even want to eat. Did you ever get totally absorbed in something so interesting and fulfilling that you actually forgot to eat? The hunger pangs came on, but you were doing something better than eating so you said, "Let the food wait." Well find something so interesting to do that you can get this message: that whatever is most interesting and valuable to YOU is what will stop you from eating. The secret of Dr. Hills Plan is that you must do it with a passion. It is fire in the belly that makes you want to eat, but it is fire in the belly for something else that will *stop* you from eating. When you find this thing, do it like you are making love. The Dr. Hills Slimming Plan is not something to be read and digested mentally; it is meant to be put into practice. It is meant to take off weight. Every part of the plan is an open door into a better life for anyone willing to walk through it. But do not expect to be carried through it. Even if that were possible, it would rob you of the fulfillment of having done it yourself. The diet will work for you because it is really easy to stick to it.

Integrity not only means doing what you say you will do. An integral person is one whose thoughts and feelings are also the same as his words and actions. Such a person has strength and feels good with himself. Once you decide to be integral, you will be careful what you set yourself to do, because you'll know that once you say it, you're going to follow through. Only a braggart is going to make a big production out of dieting and aim for results that he has not the ability to reach. He has already enjoyed his reward in the fanfare of starting, whereas a person who really means to lose the weight will start with more modest goals and will be rewarded not only by results but by a feeling of worth.

One man used to write out each new diet in beautiful penmanship and frame it like a picture and hang it on the kitchen wall. He would go over each menu with his wife so that she could see that he had the foods he had designated for each meal. His spirits were high and he felt optimistic and determined. This time would be different! But having finished the meals his wife prepared, he would add a few extras—perhaps a piece of bread or a bit of cracker and cheese or even a candy. The next month he would write out another new diet in perfect penmanship and put it in a frame and hang it in the kitchen. As a businessman he was a man of his word, but as a dieter he "cheated". Why? He was quite serious about losing weight, but he was not serious about integrity. He made his wife responsible for his diet and that meant that if she didn't catch him sneaking extras, he had gotten away with it. But the pain of getting on the scales and finding no change in his weight, in spite of all the cottage cheese, was his own pain, not hers.

Why haven't you lost the weight before? If it is so easy to do, why has it taken so long? Perhaps it is because you did not accept the responsibility yourself but put all the burden on the system or diet book you were using. Maybe you just wolfed down whatever the book said you could have, even though the books are often deceptive, promising what you should *not* have, so that more copies of the book will sell to self-deceptive people who would never have been overweight in the first place had they not been expert rationalizers. Now you must become an anti-rationalizer. You and you alone will be responsible for the state of your consciousness and the size of your body. If you make the choice to try this Slimming Plan, you are undertaking nothing less than selfmastery, and if you afterward toss it aside and go back to your old ways, you will soon be twice the size you were before you started, because you will have betrayed your own commitment, and this is different from any diet plan you may have tried before. I am asking that you become responsible, not only for your weight but for your life, and I suggest that you do not even begin this plan unless you are really in earnest. If you are merely trying to avoid being fat, you may eat three pieces of pizza when you should only eat one. But once you take responsibility for your thinness as well as your fatness, you will begin to obey the laws of eating. The first law of the stomach is to eat only until you are three-quarters full, then stop eating. This is an ancient law of yoga, and it *works*! You will soon discover the magic of it, but at first you must do it on faith. By the time you finish dieting with this Plan you will not only be slim, you will be a totally different person. Of course, this promise only holds if you do make the decision once and for all at a deep level, to change. If you do that, all the laws of the universe will back you in your efforts, and more strength than you have ever had before will come to you from within, because you will be aligned with who you really are, instead of who you wish you were or think you should be or believe you have always been. All that is real is this Self which can take the power of its own consciousness and work a miracle, for no other reason than the simple fact that it decided to do so. I have done this many times myself, so I am not just setting impossible challenges for you without understanding your difficulties. The decision to change is never easy, but it is far easier than trying to lose weight without having even *made* that decision. This is impossible and is painfully difficult, as you well know. The real decision is simple and is rather like scaling a mountain. Once you have your grappling hook firmly secured, the climb itself is easy. Normally the initial decision to diet is the easy part and everything thereafter is hard work. But this is because you have decided to "take off fat" which is a negative and incomplete motivation, very different from a decision to be master of oneself at many levels, including the level of the physical body. There is a certain negative feeling about oneself when one is only trying to take off fat. It is a feeling of apology which says: "I am a weakling, as you can see. That's how I gained all this weight. Now I am struggling to take some of it off and this is rather embarrassing, since I am still the same sort of person as before and really would love to just stuff myself with goodies. I hate having you see me in this predicament of wrestling with these unmastered desires." The real decision to change and to take your life in your own hands and to take the responsibility for being slender puts your dieting in an entirely different framework. It says, "Yes, I know I got myself in this condition, but you won't see me here for long, because I'm different now." Since it was your consciousness that created the overweight body in the first place, you have total certainty that your new state of consciousness is going to create something quite different. If your friends and family do not think so, they will see soon enough just how wrong they are. Every overweight person has within them the capacity to make this choice. Don't let anyone tell you you haven't the strength. *Do it now*, before you read any further. Make this decision, because this choice is the most important ingredient in the Dr. Hills Slimming Plan. Without it, you may as well give up before you start. With it, you can discover a new you.

REMEMBER

* You have the power to completely transform your life and be the person you've always wanted to be.

* The secret of the Dr. Hills Slimming Plan is to alternate "free days" when you can eat any food you like, without guilt, and "shape up days", when you eat no meals but take in the nutrients you need to burn away fat, yet without being hungry or losing your energy.

* On your "free days", you fill your stomach only three-quarters full, to allow the stomach room to churn the food.

* Thoughts, feelings, and attitudes create the external situations of our lives, including overweight. You can change the external by changing the way you use your consciousness.

* You can draw forth your potential as a unique person while your slender body is also emerging from its covering of fat.

* If you *practice* the principles of the Dr. Hills Slimming Plan, you will not only be slim but will be a totally different person.

* Your success depends not upon kinds of foods or quantities of foods but on a real desire, willingness and firm *decision* to change.

RULES

There are very few rules in the Dr. Hills Slimming Plan, and they are based on common sense.

1. Eat what you like on your "free day", except avoid fatty things like cream cakes and mayonnaise.
2. Never make yourself feel guilty by cheating on your "shape up days" but eat the Light Force nutritious snacks and supplements to keep your energy up.
3. Don't overload your system but always leave your stomach only three-quarters full.
4. Drink all your liquids on your "free days" *before* meals, when you take your Fiber-Lean, not with the meals. Drink plenty of liquids and water and juices but *not with food*. Drink thirty minutes before or two hours after eating.
5. Remember, many commercially prepared drinks are just concentrated sugar. Even a glass of grape juice or apple juice gives you four to six teaspoons of sugar.
6. On your "shape up days" you can take plenty of liquids with your supplements and Nibblesticks.
7. Don't eat junk foods, otherwise known as convenience foods. You can substitute for them plenty of green vegetables, grains, beans and Galactomannan Nibblesticks.
8. Exercise, preferably in a way that you enjoy.
9. Use a minimum of salt. Salt increases appetite.
10. When consciousness changes, the body also changes.

INTRODUCING DR. HILLS 100% SPIRULINA

For years there have been products on the market that could curb hunger by chemical means, but this meant that dieters had to pay a price in subjecting their bodies to chemicals in order to stave off the pressure of hunger while dieting. If you go into a drugstore and look at the diet-aid counter, you will see how few natural ingredients are in the products which are sold to dieters. It was not quite the same with "starch blockers", a natural product extracted from red kidney beans. It was claimed that you did away with starch by inhibiting it with an enzyme. It was eat and enjoy what you like. And why not, if you can stay healthy? But who knows for sure? The Food and Drug Administration does not agree with starch blockers because they say the claims have not been proved.

Light Force Company does not follow the untested methods but bases its diet plan on a food which has been eaten for centuries, even going back to the times of the Aztecs. Now, with Spirulina, it is possible to deal with the pain of hunger naturally—with a food. Spirulina is a food, a vegetable plankton which has in some cultures of the world been used as a staple food for centuries. Because it is concentrated and nutritious, even a little of it makes you feel you have had a complete meal. This enables you to miss a meal if you need to or to take in half as much food as usual without getting hungry later on in the day or running out of energy.

Here is what one Doctor of Chiropractic and pharmacist wrote about his experience of Spirulina:

> Before becoming familiar with Spirulina, I utilized the high fiber diet for years to normalize weight in my overweight patients. Although generally satisfied with the results, there were some patients whose food cravings wouldn't allow them to remain on the regimen. With the addition of Spirulina however, this has ceased to be a problem.
>
> Dr. Don Osborn
> from the book, *Inside-Out Nutritional Plan* (1981)

Of course, most overweight people are overweight because they *love the taste of food,* so some have tried to keep their same food intake and add Spirulina to it, hoping it will have some magic effect. They gain more weight and say that Spirulina doesn't work. They are right. Spirulina only works for people who can remember that they have more than the one goal of eating. You may want to eat and you may enjoy eating, but you also want to be slender. This produces a conflict in most diet plans. But with Dr. Hills' plan, you enjoy both without feeling guilty. Spirulina offers you both, because of the structure of alternating "free days" and "shape up days". On your "shape up days" you eat Spirulina and other Light Force diet products so that *on your "free days" you can eat anything you like without gaining weight.* And you can do this without any concern over nutrition, because Spirulina is one of the most nutritious foods in existence, and the other supplements are made from the finest quality natural sources —no chemical concoctions or anything that will fool your palate while shortchanging your body.

SPIRULINA: What It Is and What It Isn't
AN INTERVIEW WITH DR. HILLS

Q: Why is Spirulina the most essential dietary ingredient of your Slimming Plan?

A: Because its proteins and rare carbohydrates, like rhamnose and plant glycogen, give quicker energy than more common carbohydrates and fattening ingredients usually give.

Q: Will Spirulina really suppress appetite as some people claim that it will?

A: It is not like a chemical pill which acts as an appetite suppressor. It is so chock full of nutrients that your body feels and knows it is satisfied. Even animals know this when they eat Spirulina. Just try it out on them!

Q: How does Spirulina compare with other high-protein foods?

A: Spirulina is not only the most highly concentrated known natural protein in the world, it is also an efficient protein, quite different from other proteins. It is a biliprotein, and that means a similar protein to blood or liver proteins.

Q: Some people lose weight with Spirulina and some apparently do not. How do you account for that?

A: If you don't cheat and you stay on Spirulina, you will soon come to your correct weight. It may take a period of adjustment. A rare few will even gain a bit at first before their metabolism normalizes and then they will begin to lose weight. We have even tried Spirulina out on old tired, fat and flabby dogs. They have become young and active again.

Q: Why is Spirulina so high in price?

A: There are not many sources of Spirulina as yet in the world, but there is a large demand, which makes for high prices. The Mexican suppliers have taken advantage of this in their policy of jacking up their price 300% and not sticking to our original marketing concept. When we get more production of Spirulina, the price will go down.

Q: Is Spirulina safe and will it work for people who are overweight due to special metabolic problems?

A: Nothing is "safe" for everyone, because each individual is different. Spirulina has been eaten safely for centuries by various civilizations, and the United Nations Industrial Development Organization (a division of the United Nations) commissioned and published a five-year toxicology study on Spirulina, finding it nontoxic. Nevertheless, if you have any unique problems of any kind, you would have to consult your doctor before trying any new food or supplement.

Q: Do you personally eat Spirulina and do you and Mrs. Hills believe in it?

A: Yes, we eat Spirulina, although we are both so healthy that neither of us has ever had a major disease. I believe that eating Spirulina is to eat the most concentrated food on the planet. It would be cheap even at double the present price. If you work out its profile, it can save money. For myself, I believe I can live on the equivalent of $1.50 worth of Spirulina a day. I don't know any other food protein which costs this little, when you take digestibility and quality into account. We have records of people who have lived eight months on a diet of Spirulina, fruit juices, Fiber-Lean dietary fibers, and Light Force supplements, having their blood tested ˜regularly by doctors at a Sacramento hospital.

Q: Why do you recommend Spirulina?

A: My approach to health is prevention rather than cure. I don't wait 'til I am old and sick before I begin to take positive action. That's why I take ginseng and Spirulina and a full complement of vitamins every day. This is the basis of our Slimming Plan too. The time to do something about your future body is now. If you keep putting if off, you will never have what you want most, i.e., abundant health and a loveable body. There are some people who feel that life is not worth living if they cannot eat as much as they like of the things they enjoy. One woman who was ill and was put on a diet even said to her friend, "If I can't eat, what's the point of living?" Not only had she been abusing her body but she had narrowed her view of life down to the pleasures of eating, not even wanting to hear that there are other joys in life besides eating. Our bodies are instruments given us for a short time so that we can fulfill ourselves in many ways, but to enjoy life to the full we have to have strong, agile and active bodies. If we can look at Spirulina as a "manna from heaven", as a way of energizing the body, we can in a short while rejuvenate ourselves and demonstrate that we value the wonderful gift of a perfectly functioning body.

Your Body Will Tell You How It Feels About Spirulina

Spirulina is so packed with protein, vitamins, minerals, cell salts, and enzymes, it is the most concentrated natural form of nutrition you can buy. It is grown by the action of sunlight on water and is in fact a form of trapped sunlight. With Spirulina, more than with most vegetables, you are ingesting vital life-giving energy, because Spirulina concentrates the sun's light into chlorophyll-containing tissues at many times the growth rate of any land-grown plant. In addition to chlorophyll and beta carotene, Spirulina also contains another fantastic pigment called phycocyanin, the source of Vitamin B-12. One reason Spirulina has such a wide range of nutrients is because it is not dependent on soils depleted by years of farming. It grows in very alkaline lakes and ponds which are heavily saturated with minerals.

Spirulina growing ponds.

The minerals are so concentrated in Spirulina ponds that very little else can live in the water except the little spirals of Spirulina plankton. These minerals can be absorbed and assimilated easily by humans and animals, whereas the *in*organic minerals added by commercial manufacturers to vitamin products are often nutritionally worthless because they are hardly assimilated at all and are rejected by the body.

Spirulina is especially appreciated by people with low blood sugar (hypoglycemia), because they find it hard to diet without upsetting the delicate balance of their blood sugar. Spirulina allows them to put in the needed food without the unwanted weight gain. You can enjoy your breakfast and your lunch and then in the evening several days a week, let your supper be Spirulina. This is only one of the ways that you can use Spirulina as a diet aid. You can find the way that best suits you. If you substitute Spirulina for all or part of a meal, you will feel not stuffed but quite full, because its high quality nutrients and pigments are rapidly assimilated into your bloodstream, producing immediate feelings of fullness as well as some long-term benefits you didn't even count on.

As with any new food, you may need to give your body a little time to adjust to it. You should start with a small amount at first. Also you need to remember it is a very concentrated food and you'll need to take plenty of liquid with it. You can take it in tablet form or use the powder in soups, smoothies, or in your vegetables, salads, etc. If you have the real 100% Spirulina (not imitations) and you use it rightly, you will soon discover for yourself its effects on your metabolism.

Its proteins are biliproteins, which normally would have to be made in the liver. Spirulina contains pigments* ready-made and ready to go to work. Most proteins use up so much energy in the process of being converted to usable energy that people turn instead to carbohydrates for their energy because they can feel the difference. They feel an immediate lift in energy. But carbohydrates do not provide the tissue-building nutrition of amino acids and they can clog the system with excess calories. This is why Spirulina is such a marvelous gift for dieters, because with just the few calories in Spirulina you are nourished and satisfied and have the

---

*These organic pigments like chlorophyll, heme, bilirubin, carotenoids, and phyco-cyanin are not to be confused with the inorganic mineral pigment contained in paint.

quick energy you used to think you had to get from high-calorie carbohydrates. Its exceptional protein is lower in calories than other proteins and, according to many hundreds of letters received from all over America, it is higher in energy production than any other known food.

Most dieters know all about grams and calories and quantitative methods of losing weight. But they know very little about qualitative methods. Even professional nutritionists are generally ignorant of the difference in quality between one kind of protein and another or one kind of carbohydrate and another. Scientific research on the role of biological pigments in our bodies is only just beginning, and yet the pigments produced by the liver in the process of metabolism are crucial to our health and are miraculous helpers for anyone who wants to lose weight. Spirulina plankton is not only rich in high-quality protein pigments but also in high-quality carbohydrates, as well as a vast array of naturally chelated vitamins and minerals. This is why such a small amount of this concentrated high-nutrition food can serve as a meal or half of a meal.

It is no use going on the Dr. Hills Slimming Plan and talking about Spirulina as a sacrifice of other foods. Spirulina is the king of foods in its own right. You must tune in to what Spirulina gives you, not what it takes away. If you knew it had all the properties to make you young and vital, would you not only take it every day but take it and watch the fat disappear? But human nature is not made that way. Human nature is so stubborn, contrary and self-defeating, but it doesn't need to be. Spirulina has changed all that for thousands of people. The problem is that other thousands have never eaten the real thing. Many people trust the health food stores, but how do store buyers know what the manufacturer put in the products? They don't, and that is a fact. Spirulina is in limited supply so the chances of getting the real thing are small. If you tried a brand other than Dr. Hills', you may have felt nothing, because the manufacturers themselves cannot be sure that the Spirulina has not been cut or adulterated with alfalfa or green vegetable powder. This means you must insist on purity to get the right result and not blame the Spirulina if you bought an unscrupulous brand which says 100% but is really 2%. Spirulina is good for you in several ways but the main advantage is its unbeatable metabolic pigments.

Spirulina is also a complete protein. If you eat protein which is lacking in certain of the amino acids (i.e., is incomplete), then some of the amino acids that you *did* ingest are eliminated by the body, because the body has to have several different kinds of amino acids present simultaneously to form the building blocks of the tissues. So even though you may have eaten protein and you may even have digested and assimilated it well, you still may not retain it for use by the body. With Spirulina there is no such worry; it has all the amino acids needed for optimum health. However, if you *only* compare the Spirulina amino acids with the same amino acids in other foods—for example in calculating the Net Protein Utilization (NPU)—then you are again leaving out the factors which make Spirulina unique among foods.

There are skeptics about everything and several skeptics have been quoted saying that Spirulina has no more value than chicken liver or peanuts. Be assured that these people know nothing about the real value of Spirulina. Challenge them to start using Spirulina on a regular basis because many of these people have never even seen it, let alone researched its properties or pigments. But make sure their opinion is based on the right brand of Spirulina and insist on personal and tested knowledge and not theory. You must try it to believe it, and once you try it out, you won't need to ask the opinion of anyone else.

REMEMBER

* Spirulina makes it possible to diet without hunger. It is so concentrated and nutritious that even a little of it is like a meal.

* Whereas many diets make it possible to cut down food by supplying chemicals or man-made nutrients, Spirulina is a *food*—both natural and extremely nutritious.

* Start with a small amount of Spirulina to give your body time to get used to something new.

* Because Spirulina is concentrated, you will need to drink extra liquid when you take it.

* Due to its amazing biological pigments, Spirulina is quickly assimilated and, if you have genuine 100% Spirulina, you will be able to feel its effects.

* Spirulina is a plant, very high in complete protein and is one of Nature's richest sources of Vitamin B-12.

INTRODUCING FIBER-LEAN ™

Unique Fiber-Lean is an incredible help to those who want to lose weight, because (with only 22 calories per tablespoon) it fills you up so you don't feel like eating more. No more pressure from compulsive desires to snack between meals; your appetite is satisfied by Fiber-Lean, yet it is not making you fat. On the contrary, this remarkable fiber is helping to clean your intestinal tract just like a scrub brush, so it is helping you lose weight in two ways at once, plus there is a third benefit—its excellent nutrition.

* Just by eating Fiber-Lean before each meal, you can achieve gradual weight loss without even changing your diet and it will help you lose even faster when you use it in this carefully planned Slimming Program!

* Fiber-Lean absorbs excess fats, toxic wastes, and bile acids in your intestine. Normally these would leach into the bloodstream, but Fiber-Lean—your intestinal scrub brush —pushes them through the intestine and out of the body. Your body will feel a tremendous difference, once this process is under way.

* Bran, glucomannan, and other fibers offer little in the way of nutrition, whereas Fiber-Lean is high in protein, so you feel nourished as well as full. It is high in many amino acids, with a Protein Efficiency Ratio (P.E.R.) of 2.5, higher than casein, which is what most protein powders are made from.

Why Do You Need Fiber?

The most common cause of obesity lies in the consumption of refined carbohydrates. Most people believe that they are overweight because they have a large appetite or because they dislike exercise. This is not true. It is true that restraining the appetite and enforcing exercise will reduce obesity, but the true cause of any weight problem is the consumption of too many refined carbohydrates and too many fats. Primitive man had fiber in his diet, and this was his natural protection from obesity. He had to chew his food more than we do, with our refined sugars and starches from which the fiber has been removed. The fiber and the chewing made him feel full, even though he may have eaten only a medium amount of food, whereas we who are eating refined food must eat an abnormally large amount before we get the feeling of satisfaction. The reason you feel full after eating Fiber-Lean is that it increases the bulk of matter in your stomach for a longer period of time before it passes to the intestine. It does not dissolve in the stomach but passes into the small intestine.

Here Is How It Works

Fiber-Lean absorbs ten times its bulk in liquid, so you take a large glass of water or juice with it. The fiber then forms into a slippery jelly in the intestine, which makes you feel full of food. It also makes you regular and stimulates the intestines, and it absorbs mucous as well as liquids. The jelly-like substance increases the fiber content of the feces, softens and helps expel it. With good elimination, wastes don't pile up, and you feel clean. This speedy elimination also gives your body less time to absorb dietary cholesterol. Fiber in the diet has actually been proven to reduce the amount of serum blood cholesterol in the body. Meanwhile, you are eating the foods you like but you eat less, so fiber helps you cut down your calories without drastically cutting your eating, and you never feel empty or hungry. The fiber gives your intestine the bulk it needs for fast, easy assimilation of nutrients and, when mixed with high energy-giving foods, high vitamins, minerals and protein in Spirulina, Fiber-Lean is a great basis for any slimming plan.

Health Benefits

The galactomannans in Fiber-Lean are known to help eliminate harmful chemicals in the intestine (e.g., if you have been on valium, tranquilizers, drugs, antibiotics), and it may serve as an antacid buffer as well. The *Senate Select Committee on Nutrition and Human Needs* in 1977 pointed out a crucial correlation between obesity, modern-day diseases, and lack of dietary fiber. And this was one of its greatest concerns. The committee's report warns that lack of dietary fiber in the modern diet is a prominent cause of most degenerative diseases, either directly or indirectly. Since the processed and refined food industries have almost completely eliminated our fiber intake, it is easy for us to become obese and to open ourselves to the danger of high blood pressure, heart disease, arteriosclerosis and many other digestive organ diseases, including cancer of the colon and of the rectum. We do not make the statement that fiber will *cure* such conditions, but there is evidence that it can help to prevent them. There are societies in Africa, rural areas where *high* fiber diets are eaten, in which people suffer much less from such diseases, especially diabetes, which often may be related to too little fiber.

At The Technion (Israel Institute of Technology), the Faculty of Medicine has done considerable research which shows that So-Bit (from which Fiber-Lean is made) can reduce the amount of insulin needed by diabetics by lowering sugar content in their blood. Galactomannans, which are found in Fiber-Lean, do this more effectively than do glucomannans. The fiber slows down the sugar glucose absorption in the body, stabilizing and lowering blood glucose levels. Dr. Yoram Kanter*, head of the research team and Diabetes Service and Research Unit at Rambam Hospital, reports, "We don't claim that it replaces insulin, but taken in small quantities, it reduces the 'after meals' glucose response that diabetics develop which otherwise leads to a rise in sugar content". The diet used at Rambam Hospital improved the insulin responses also in the obese. For the ordinary person, Fiber-Lean helps stabilize the blood glucose level, because it slows the rate of sugar absorption in your body. This means that you don't feel ups and downs in your energy level, which make you want to snack and eat more.

To sum up the health benefits of Fiber-Lean:**
- It can help eliminate harmful chemicals in the intestine
- It can serve as an antacid buffer
- It can help prevent modern degenerative conditions
- It can lower the sugar content in the blood of obese people and diabetics, hence reducing the need for as much insulin. It does this by slowing the rate of sugar absorption, which means a more stable energy level and fewer ups and downs or craving for a snack.

---

*Reference to Dr. Kanter's work is a paper presented last year at the annual meeting of the American Diabetes Association in Washington D.C. The paper described research conducted by Rambam Hospital Department of Internal Medicine, headed by Professor David Barzilai, reporting a significant lowering of glucose levels both in diabetics and in the obese, through the soya fiber diet.

**This soy fiber we call Fiber-Lean must not be confused with the fiber left over from milling the hulls of the beans, which has many nutritional disadvantages and is usually thrown away. Fiber-Lean is made by a complicated process of extraction from the cotyledon from which all antinutrients have been removed, leaving a 40%–60% protein fiber coupled with 30%–50% complex carbohydrate fibers such as galactomannans, which are superior fibers to glucomannans.

The health benefits of Fiber-Lean are first a result of its capacity to fill us up while at the same time making our nutrient absorption more efficient, and second a result of its dynamic cleansing action which can be felt by anyone very soon after beginning to use Fiber-Lean. Once we begin to get rid of the toxic wastes that we habitually carry around in our intestinal tract, we feel a feeling of lightness which is the opposite of the feeling of having eaten a big meal (which should provide more energy but doesn't). It is as if we have had a very light meal and yet feel brighter and more full of pep.

CHAPTER 5

OUTLINE OF DR. HILLS SLIMMING PROGRAM

The program is divided into alternating "free days" and "shape up days". On your "free day" you use nutritious diet supplements to lessen your appetite and you can eat any food you like except foods with fat. On your "shape up day" you take no meals but instead eat specific diet supplements to curb your appetite. Each "free day" is followed by a "shape up day" with three free days and four shape up days per week.

PLAN A

Free Day

On your "free day" take the following supplements in addition to your meals:

Up to 3 level teaspoons of Fiber-Lean*
in milk, juice, or soup
2 or more tablets of 100% Spirulina
2 tablets of OB-1
} **Three times a day: half an hour before meals**

1 tablet of Wildfire** *after* every meal
} **Three times a day: after meals**

1 tablet of ZMS Boost (no more than 1 per day)
Lecithin Smoothie (with Spirulina Powder or
Manna Powder optional) Use 1 tablespoon of
LecithinPLUS.
} **Once a day**

A smoothie*** is a luscious drink made by putting your favorite beautiful in-season fresh fruits in a blender with juice and whipping them up into a thick naturally sweet healthful treat. You can use apples, bananas, pears, strawberries, blackberries, blueberries, plums, peaches, nectarines or any fruit you like. (In winter you can add a few frozen fruits if there are fewer fresh fruits available.)

On your free day, eat Ram Bam Bread instead of bread.

---

*Once your body gets used to Fiber-Lean as a new ingredient in your diet, you can increase the amount up to one level tablespoon three times a day. Some people are happy with one level tablespoon before meals, and very overweight people can take up to two tablespoons three times a day. You must experiment by gradually increasing the amount, but remember, the more you take, the more liquids you will need, and the same is true of Spirulina.

**Some people experience a brief heat rush from the niacin in Wildfire and may prefer to take just one a day.

***Apple juice, pineapple and grape juice have double the fattening power of other juices, so decrease the quantity when using these juices. See Part II for smoothie recipes and delicious soup recipes.

Plan A (cont.)

Shape Up Day

At any time during your shape up day, you can munch on Dr. Hills Galactomannan Nibblesticks.

EAT AS MANY AS YOU LIKE!

BREAKFAST:

Start the day with a luscious fruit smoothie containing 1 tablespoon of Lecithin^{Plus}. (Addition of 100% Spirulina Powder or Manna Powder is optional).

2 tablets of OB-1
2 tablets of Garlic Spirulina
1 tablet of Tienchi Boost*
2 or more tablets of 100% Spirulina (if you have not put Spirulina in your smoothie)
1 tablespoon of Bee Sweet Pollen

MIDMORNING ENERGY BOOST:

1–2 Wildfire** tablets together with
2 tablets of Green Gold

LUNCH:

Spirulina or Manna Powder Smoothie (1 level tablespoon of 100% Spirulina Powder*** or Manna Powder in a fruit juice or vegetable juice smoothie)
2 tablets of Garlic Spirulina
2 tablets of OB-1
2 or more tablets of 100% Spirulina (if you have not put Spirulina in your smoothie)

---

*Tienchi ginseng—The Pearl of Chinese Medicine—researched by government medical and pharmaceutical heart specialists. Researched by the Peking Institute of Physical Culture in control of body weight.

**Some people experience a brief heat rush from the niacin in Wildfire and may prefer to take just one a day.

***First accustom your body to the new food, Spirulina, then eat as much as you want of it, in place of other foods; it will nourish your body while making your dieting easier.

Plan A, Shape Up Day
Lunch (cont.)

1 tablet of Tienchi Boost (optional)
1 tablespoon of Bee Sweet Pollen

(If it is winter, you may prefer to substitute hot drinks in your smoothies, using broth, bouillon, warm cider, or warm vegetable juices.)

MIDAFTERNOON ENERGY BOOST:

1-2 tablets of Wildfire with 2 tablets of Green Gold

DINNER:

2 tablets of OB-1
2 tablets of Garlic Spirulina
1 tablet of ZMS Boost (no more than 1 per day)
2 or more tablets of 100% Spirulina
1 tablet of Tienchi Boost (optional)
1 tablespoon of Bee Sweet Pollen

BEFORE BED:

1 tablet of Tienchi Boost

PLAN B
(Budget)

(Plan B is designed to cut expenditures as your budget will permit.)

Free Day

On your "Free Day" take the following supplements:

Up to 3 level teaspoons of Fiber-Lean ⎫   **Three times:**
  in milk, juice or soup*   ⎬ **half an hour**
2 or more tablets of 100% Spirulina   ⎭ **before meals**
2 tablets of OB-1

1 tablet of Tienchi Boost** ⎫
1 tablet of ZMS Boost   ⎬ **Once a day**
1 Lecithin Smoothie (with fruit or fruit juice)
  Use 1 tablespoon of Lecithin^{PLUS}. ⎭

On your free day, eat Ram Bam Bread instead of bread.

Shape Up Day

At any time during your shape up day, you can munch on Dr. Hills Galactomannan Nibblesticks.

EAT AS MANY AS YOU LIKE!

BREAKFAST:

Start the day with a luscious fruit smoothie containing 1 tablespoon of Lecithin^{PLUS}. (Addition of 100% Spirulina Powder*** or Manna Powder is optional)
2 tablets of OB-1
2 or more tablets of 100% Spirulina
1 tablespoon of Bee Sweet Pollen

---

*Once your body gets used to Fiber-Lean as a new ingredient in your diet, you can increase the amount if you need to. You should increase your intake of fluids as you increase the amount of Fiber-Lean.

**Tienchi ginseng—The Pearl of Chinese Medicine—researched by government medical and pharmaceutical heart specialists. Researched by the Peking Institute of Physical Culture in control of body weight.

***First accustom your body to the new food, Spirulina, and then increase the amount.

LUNCH:

Spirulina Powder or Manna Powder Smoothie (1 level tablespoon
of 100% Spirulina Powder or Manna Powder in a fruit juice or
vegetable juice smoothie)
2 tablets of OB-1
2 or more tablets of 100% Spirulina
1 tablespoon of Bee Sweet Pollen

(If it is winter, you may prefer to substitute hot drinks in your
smoothies, using broth, bouillon, warm cider or warm vegetable
juice.)

DINNER:

2 tablets of OB-1
1 tablet of ZMS Boost (no more than 1 per day)
2 or more tablets of 100% Spirulina
1 tablespoon of Bee Sweet Pollen

BEFORE BED:

1 tablet of Tienchi Boost

On embarking on this diet you may find that you begin a
heavy cleansing with different bowel reactions for the first
three days. This is normal as the body begins to adjust. If there
is constipation, you may take more liquids or a mild herbal
laxative. By the fourth day, you should be feeling fantastic and
energetic. Here are some of the comments of people who
have reached day four and gone beyond:

6th day: "It seems like the toxins have come out of my body
and the elimination process is easing up. I feel GREAT today."
V. Konttinen
4th day: "The first two days weren't so hot, but now, my
fourth day, feels great! My second shape up day took off three
pounds." B. Ford

2nd and 3rd day: "On my second day I stayed up 'til 1:30 a.m. and got up four and one-half hours later and felt fine. The next night I stayed up until 12:45 and got up four and one-half hours later and woke up with a BOING—clear-headed and energetic and I felt absolutely fantastic. I feel irrepressibly energetic. I feel like jumping and running. There has been an enormous change in my health." P. Osborn

3rd day: "The first shape up day my energy level was pretty low, didn't feel too good. The rest of the days my energy has been picking up and I feel energetic and clear. I LOVE TIENCHI—the energy I get from it is very balanced and calm, but it keeps me moving." L. Hengstebeck

8th day: "Well-being and energy level fantastic. Never been so high. Using Tienchi I feel tremendous regenerative effects— two tabs before bedtime." R. Welker

4th day: "Well-being and energy level about 200% better." R. Smith

WHAT DO PEOPLE LIKE ABOUT THE PROGRAM?

"I like the discipline and challenge of doing the program. I like the clarity of mind and the feeling of being healthy." L.H.

"Creates will." R.W.

"Every other day makes it easy." S.G.

"Challenge to self-discipline! (Didn't work, though. I haven't got the discipline.)" V.K.

"I've lost weight, plus the alternating of eating/fasting is good." J.G.

"Freedom to eat the foods I like." D.E.

"I feel full after the drink with Spirulina, Lecithin, and Fiber-Lean. It quells the appetite."   B.F.

"The assurance of super-nutrition and the boost from TIENCHI."
                                                                                                                 W.R.

"I like the Fiber-Lean Spirulina combination."   P.O.

REMEMBER

* Will power alone is not enough.
* Spirulina, Fiber-Lean and Light Force Supplements make you feel filled full.
* Find out what will make you feel fulfilled.
* When consciousness changes, the body also changes.
* Alternating "free" and "shape up" days make it easy to win by losing.

NOTE: If you are a compulsive eater and you gorge yourself on Ram Bam Bread or Nibblesticks incessantly, then "Eat All You Like" does not apply to you, because you will soon develop a problem by not having consumed enough liquid. If you cannot stop nibbling, then you should limit yourself to six (1½ oz.) Ram Bam buns or ten Nibblesticks per day.

THE LAW OF BALANCE

The basic principle of Dr. Hills Slimming Plan is balance. For example, if you tend to like noodles instead of lettuce, then you will need to balance that tendency by making sure your body's need for roughage and health-building nutrients is met. To do this, you will have three "free days" and four "shape up" balance days. On the "shape up days" you will eat Dr. Hills' special diet supplements ONLY. On free days, you will use specific supplements *in addition* to your noodles or whatever you choose to eat. But this is not a license to gorge on "free days", even though you are free to do so if you choose. Your results will be more rewarding if you splurge only now and then but use most free days just to enjoy normal eating. There is a difference between enjoyment and an orgy, and you can feel the difference psychologically. Though you might lose weight in spite of excesses on free days, you still will not feel good about yourself, and that is the whole point of being slender in the first place, isn't it? Your "shape up day" is the day you feel good with yourself because you are shaping your worth as well as your body.

No shopping at the store for special foods worrying what to eat. On your "shape up day" you eat only the supplements recommended, and this will balance whatever you ate yesterday. It is best not to upset the balance by taking all your "free days" at once and then living on the diet aids for four days in a row. Hold to the pattern of alternation, not rigidly, but as much as you can, because it is based on a law of metabolism. If the body gets nutrients one day, it can use them for metabolizing on two days, so that every other day (alternate days) eating excellent nutrition will keep it running well.

The reason for taking supplements on your "free day" as well as on your "shape up day" is to help you feel full and nourished so you only take a reasonable amount of your favorite foods. This way it is easy and you don't have to count any calories or weigh yourself every day; you just follow the law of balance. On your "free day" you can eat any food you like except those known to contain fats, such as:

* French fries and the batter on the outside of fried chicken
* Thick sauces, butter, gravies, and dressings like mayonnaise
* Cakes, cookies, ice cream (unless made with nonfat dairy or soy products)

But you must remember on your "free day" to leave one-fourth of your stomach empty to give room for the churning of your food in the digestive process. This helps the food to get through the colon quicker, making you more regular.

The supplements can cut your grocery bills by forty percent, but before you begin to buy anything at all, I must tell you how with these aids you can lose weight and feel great. You can eliminate fatigue and provide energy through a unique combination of high-energy mental techniques along with the healthful natural ingredients in these Light Force products. Remember that human nutrition is still poorly understood. If it were not so, everyone would be thin. If you are an eater and you restrain yourself, you may set up a stress which will make your dieting obsessive. If you try to self-starve yourself or try hard to control your eating, you will build up pressure and eventually burst out in a fit of eating. You must control the *cause* of your eating habits, not the effect. If you focus on the effect that you want—namely to become thin—you may try, as most dieters do, to be disciplined and say no. But saying no when your craving says yes is no good in this plan. That produces emotional stress which indirectly raises fatty acids in the body.

The affluent society of ease and labor-saving devices and tempting food exposes us to environmental temptations which help us to gain weight. But your contempt of your pounds will make you feel unhappy, unloved and unwanted. Therefore you have to watch your philosophy as much as you watch your fat.

Everyone can learn how to lose weight but the real trick is how to hold on to your losses when you have got them off. All dieters have had some success in losing weight but very few can keep the weight off for more than a few weeks. This is where you go onto a regular nutrition plan using Light Force products to keep your figure slender and to keep your success in weight loss. With Dr. Hills' plan, you lose to win. You get immediate results, but please allow yourself three months (12 weeks) to finish the job. Realize that wishing for a quick result may make you wait a discouragingly long time before getting to the size and shape you want to be. Therefore separate your big, big goal of getting rid of all your fat into smaller goals that are more manageable. Your "free days" allow you to eat freely anything you like without fat in it, because over the long term of three days on your favorite foods and four days on Dr. Hills' nutritious supplements, you take if off a little at a time. Three months later you are your thin self again and you keep it that way with Light Force supplements which are so packed with nutrition you don't need or even want excess.

But the first and most difficult step in the Dr. Hills Slimming Plan is to make up your mind that you will take only the recommended products on your "shape up day". You switch from your favorite food, eaten on three days a week, to energy-boosting Light Force products for four days a week. There are no rigid rules except the three-quarters full stomach on three days a week, with four days munching Dr. Hills Galactomannan Nibblesticks, which constantly clean your intestines with nutritious nonfattening fiber. Just when you feel hungry on your "shape up day", instead of going frantic and reaching for your favorite fattening food, you reach instead for a delicious crunchy Nibblestick. These crunchy diet sticks are like bread sticks or pretzels but they are made of a special polysaccharide fiber and protein, so you can eat as many as you like, although they are so filling, you will find that one or two of them will be enough. And of course, you must drink plenty of liquid with them, which will also limit naturally the amount that you desire. It is very important when using fiber (in Fiber-Lean, Ram Bam Bread, or Galactomannan Nibblesticks) to drink at least ten glasses of liquid per day. Water, herbal teas, or vegetable juices are the best choices of liquid. Begin with a small amount of these products, to give your body time to get used to something new, and then work up to whatever amount works best for you.

The Rewards of Discipline

When you have lost at least two-thirds of the weight you wanted to lose, you can give yourself a reward by reducing your shape up days to three and increasing your free days to four. Of course, if you discover that this causes you to stop losing or even to gain weight back again, you will have to return to the former schedule. But if you continue losing (though perhaps a little more slowly), then at some point you can try going down to two balance days per week, with five days free! Gradually you will taper off to no balance days at all because you no longer need them, and you will find that simply by taking the "free day" supplements before each meal, you have a diet you can easily stay on for the rest of your life and maintain the slender figure you have created. If ever you do begin to gain a little, you can quickly resort to one or two balance days until the weight is gone. The secret of maintaining a slim figure is to take fat off the moment you notice you've gained it, not waiting for it to become a big task. An easy way to lose a little weight is just to eat Spirulina for your evening meal on one or more nights of the week until the extra weight is gone. Once you discover the scientific principles which are at the back of the Light Force rejuvenation program, you will not only be slender (nice to look at) but will have an oomph you never had before. Thousands are actually feeling this oomph and zest for life and if you doubt it, talk to any Light Force distributor whose life has been changed dramatically by joining the Light Force Family.

With Dr. Hills Slimming Plan you will discover strength in your deeper self, which is greater than your difficulties. You learn to release this power simply by realizing that your body and your mind tend to perfectness and balance, because a mind greater than ours set up natural laws which work. If you believe this, then nothing is impossible, because you are not relying on your weakness but on your ability to tune to the real Source of power. The practice of this belief, not only during the Plan but throughout your life, determines the releasing of your hidden abilities and unlimited potential.

REMEMBER

* No matter what you eat on your "free days" three days a week, you will still lose weight if you follow the plan with Light Force Supplements.

* The supplements on your "free days" are designed to help you feel full and nourished so that you do not overeat.

* The supplements on your "shape up days" are designed to take away hunger and supply nutrients and energy, while your body burns off stored fat.

* You can eat any food on your "free day" providing it does not contain fat.

* On your "free day", leave one-fourth of your stomach empty at each meal.

* Allow three months to take off the fat; then begin a modified program that will help you easily maintain your new slenderness for the rest of your life.

* You can eat as much of the fiber products as you like without getting fat; they will help you to feel full with less food and will help you keep your intestines clean.

* Give your body time to get used to the fiber products; start at first with a small amount, and don't forget that the more fiber you take in, the more liquids you must take in. You will need at least ten glasses of liquid a day.

BACK IN TOUCH
WITH NATURE

We grow so used to our habits that often we do not realize we may be feeling less well than others feel, nor can we tell for sure that our habits are causing it. But many people who have changed their habits to build better health, testify with hindsight that they feel incredibly different. One way to upgrade your diet is to eliminate coffee, caffeinated teas, and tobacco to relieve your system of the harsh toll these stimulants can take. Another essential step is to replace highly processed foods with wholesome alternatives such as Spirulina, so that your body can begin to replace with healthier nutrients the toxins which have been stored over the years. To me, Spirulina is "green magic". You will hear lots of controversy about it because it is new to nutritionists, but in my opinion, it is the greatest discovery in the human diet in over 1000 years. Why do I believe that? Because I have seen it work with thousands of people. I am convinced that Spirulina prevents the uptake of contaminating chemicals and removes deposits absorbed in our bodies. If you are eager to speed this removal of accumulated "sludge" from your system, fasting can be an efficient tool.

Cleansing Period

In other books* I have described a method for cleansing the body of unwanted wastes consisting of a diet of juices, Spirulina and fiber from bran. Now that I have discovered a new source of galactomannan fiber that does a much better

---

*Available from University of the Trees Press, P.O. Box 66, Boulder Creek CA 95006.

job than bran or glucomannan, I would recommend Fiber-Lean instead of bran. For those who want to try it, a fast is a good way to begin this Slimming Program, using galacto-mannan fiber, Spirulina, and juices on a seven-day fast before beginning the alternating free and shape up days.

Many people have tried this method and have written me that they have undertaken fasts with great success when all other diet plans had failed them. Obviously if your system is in need of a head start into the Slimming Program, then you would benefit greatly from practicing a cleansing, though you should first get your doctor's approval. Many doctors are afraid you might not get enough vitamins if you stopped taking normal food for seven days. Although I know of absolutely no harm that has come to anyone by undertaking a fast with Spirulina, it is best to allay fears of critics so that you are not having to fend off negative statements from people who don't understand fasting and what it can do for you. For those who want an extra boost, take the supplements recommended for "shape up" days, along with the seven-day cleansing period.

However, to embark on the Dr. Hills Slimming Plan, you don't need to go into great details or worry about fasting unless you want to. Not everyone has the inclination or self-discipline to fast properly. This is in fact why this Slimming Plan has been written, to offer a slower process of gradually upgrading your old diet with a cleansing fiber and supplements which give your body a chance to adapt itself to more nutritious foods as you wean yourself from the wrong foods. Even though you begin to eat what you like at first on your "free days", you find yourself gradually not wanting the foods that you used to eat compulsively. Fasting is for people who have a great deal of control, while the "Shape Up" Slimming Program is for those who need to proceed step-by-step to stop eating the very things which are harmful to their bodies. It is reasonable and obvious that even if you eat fattening foods on three days of each week without guilt and don't eat those foods for four days of each week, you are going to be consuming four-sevenths less food. This is not only money in your pocket which you can spend on nutritious supplements instead of grocery bills, but it is also a common sense way to beat the irresistible urge to overeat and to train your body naturally into better nutrition habits.

A Cleansing Reaction is Positive

Whether you decide to begin the program with a fast or whether you are just following the "shape up days" which are essentially days of fasting, you may experience a cleansing reaction. During fasting, your body diverts the energy normally used for digestion and uses it to clean and maintain its organs. As a result, the accumulated toxins will begin to leach out of your tissues into your bloodstream. Until they are eliminated, these toxins are freely circulating, which means that they can repoison your body slightly, causing reactions which vary in degree according to the state of your internal health. It is vitally important to realize that it is normal to experience discomfort while fasting, such as a headache, aching joints, diarrhea, constipation or upset stomach, but this should last only until the toxins are removed from your system.

All the fiber products in the Dr. Hills Slimming Plan (Fiber-Lean, Galactomannan Nibblesticks, and Ram Bam Bread) as well as Spirulina, Garlic Spirulina, and other recommended supplements act as powerful cleansers. So if you experience an initial few days of symptoms, these are *very positive* signs that something good is happening to change your body and get it working in a new way. (On the other hand, you must listen to your body. If such symptoms last longer than a brief period or if you feel that your body needs medical attention, seek it immediately). Getting enough rest can help reduce these symptoms, but you should also continue to exercise, since toxins are eliminated more quickly from an active body. It is also important to practice deep breathing and take warm baths, because toxins are eliminated by oxidation through the breath and through skin pores. If you can wait patiently for your body to finish its important work, you can be freed from the toxins which may be sapping your strength and be filled with a new and vital "life force". Your body will be grateful for the cleansing and you may feel more alive than you have felt in years. But some people become alarmed at the cleansing reactions that happen when they first take Spirulina and Fiber-Lean, and this is why I recommend that you begin gradually. If your body has been functioning on a poor diet or even what most people call a "normal" diet, it may at first go through symptoms that feel worse instead of better. So it is very, very important that you be aware of what is happening and do not allow yourself to get discouraged on the diet. It will work for you better than you can imagine if you give your body time to get accustomed to new ways of eating. Omitting highly toxic substances such as coffee, caffeinated teas, chocolate, tobacco, salt, and highly preserved and processed foods will make that much less for your body to have to clear out. In the first phase (perhaps four days to a week) your body will be cleaning out its sludge. In the next phase, it is forming new tissues and the body is able to feel energetic with less food. With both Spirulina and Fiber-Lean, you can start a small amount per day. If you find you have few or no cleansing reactions, you can increase the amount right away. Before beginning, be sure to check with your doctor to be sure you are not suffering from medical problems. Once you get the go-ahead, remember that there is no better weight-loss program than to help your body do what it knows how to do. Given the nutrients it needs plus the galactomannan fiber, it will work for you day and night to keep you slender, youthful and in tip-top health.

REMEMBER

* For those who would like to get a head start on the Dr. Hills Slimming Plan, you can begin with a seven-day fast, before you start the alternating "free days" and "shape up days".

* Fasting speeds the removal of stored toxins from the body.

* Whether in the initial optional seven-day fast or in the beginning experience of "shape up days", you may experience uncomfortable symptoms such as headache, diarrhea, or constipation. It is important to realize that these symptoms are normal. They are a sign that your body is cleansing itself, and they are a positive signal that something good is happening.

* If you wait for the body to finish this initial cleansing, then you will feel the effects of the new nutrients that you are putting into the body and can feel increased mental clarity, heightened senses, a feeling of well-being, and vibrant energy.

* Spirulina makes fasting easy, because you keep your energy up and you need not feel hunger.

* With both Spirulina and Fiber-Lean remember to drink plenty of liquids. It is best to begin with a small amount of fiber and increase it gradually until you find the optimum amount for your own unique body system.

THE PHILOSOPHY OF PHAT

There are certain beliefs that can psychologically destroy all your efforts at dieting. For instance, if you think that your appetite is insatiable and nothing can control it except a restricted diet of special low-calorie meals, then all your efforts at dieting are guaranteed to fail. Or if you weigh yourself every day in the belief that every ounce you take off will somehow reinforce your will to stay on the diet, then you are mistaken. Why does the Dr. Hills Slimming Plan not advise daily focusing on every ounce and calorie in order to motivate yourself to continue losing weight? Because for long-range accomplishment, it is not effective. If you lose an ounce one day but not the next or if you gain it back the next day, you can't get any enthusiasm going because it is discouraging. "Scale consciousness" is very different from the steady knowing and faith in what will work and *doing it* to get the long-term results and maintain them.

People who are obsessed with their weight loss are also the first to stop a diet on the first excuse so that long-term effects are never felt. It is not necessary to adhere strictly to a diet in order to achieve success. If you want to go to the banquet and gorge on a huge dinner, the Dr. Hills Slimming Plan allows you to do this, providing you observe the laws of balance and take only the Dr. Hills' diet supplements the next day. Alternating between what you can't resist on your "free days", with the diet supplements on the next "shape up" day keeps you on the Dr. Hills Slimming Plan because you feel successful. To feel failure leads to self-defeat and a feeling of guilt. You must begin anew without any myths inherited from previous diets which failed. Yet another failure will be ensured if you don't get rid of your myths along with your fat.

Why not enjoy a new mythology, that of the Goddess *Phat*, the ancient Egyptian goddess of slimming? She will keep an eye on your secret eating habits. Dieting is a real chore to most people, so a sense of humor is necessary to avoid getting self-righteous and stressed up.

Unconscious stress actually causes you to overeat, so this program is designed to watch your mental energy as well as watching your weight. You have about as much chance of slimming without the correct philosophy as an ancient Egyptian *phattie*. A *phattie* is a tempter who tries to defeat your devotion to the Goddess of Slimming. Really a *phattie* is the part of you that undermines everything you try to do to become your own person and not be at the mercy of food or any other external thing, person, or situation. The Goddess *Phat* is the part of you that wants to do better and not be weak or petty or lazy or anything you can't respect but to actually achieve something and feel good about who you are. In many people, it is *phattie* who sits on the throne of consciousness, while the goddess is like Cinderella among the pots and cinders; she goes unrecognized until we make up our minds to rescue her.

Phat is good-hearted and straightforward, whereas *phattie* is deceptive and destructive. One of *phattie's* tactics is to lure you into "shoulds". You "should" eat a raw carrot; you "shouldn't" eat a pastry. This of course makes you want a pastry. *Phattie* plays on your emotions to get you to attempt something that will backfire. *Phattie* does not want you to become informed or to understand how your body works, because it thrives on doubt and despair. Here it is in all its glory alongside the ancient Goddess of Slimming.

Phattie

Goddess of Phat

You can gladly pay homage to the goddess because she alone has the power to get you thin. Her main purpose in the ancient Egyptian pantheon of goddesses is to inspire you not to eat of the fruit of fatness on your free day. She frowns on certain foods that contain fat! But she does not condemn you, because she likes them too. Phat is not like some health freak who likes all those rough tasteless things that stick in your throat. The goddess likes the same favorite foods that you do, but she also has common sense and this gives her the power to say "no". She is watching over you at all times, even in secret while you down those donuts! What will please our slimming goddess will please you too, because the Goddess Phat is none other than the slim figure you have always wanted to be.

Every overweight person has his or her own philosophy of fat. Yes, fat! Nothing but the plain word—F–A–T! Whatever nice word you prefer to use for the ripples and rolls of fat on the midriff, the reality is that it got there by your own thoughts and habits. Maybe you believe that losing weight is impossible because you think it means self-denial and that this will be too hard for you to do. Or you think that people like you as you are with all your fat and, "They had better like me, because that's just the way I am!" Or the thoughts say, "I should not change because people already like me the way I am, and if I stop eating what I like, I might start some other habits like drinking, smoking or biting my nails off." Dr. Hills Philosophy of Phat is quite different. First you have to admit your needs and be receptive to other people. Don't cut yourself off in your pride and stubbornness. Be receptive. Do you know how many people react to being told about their fat with inner hostility while smiling on the outside? That reaction only makes them dig their heels in more and say to themselves, "Lay off, I will eat what I like. No one is going to tell me what to do." But the problem is that someone has to tell you, and that someone is *you*! You must see that the thoughts you are having lead to actions. But the next step is not to view the task as hopeless and impossible but to see it from a different viewpoint. That viewpoint keeps asking, "How am I really fat and will I accept my problem as a challenge rather than as a sealed fate?"

In this Slimming Plan obstacles are translated into opportunities in order to get you moving. You ask at first, "Why am I fat?" and you will get a lot of answers, but no solutions. If instead you ask, "HOW am I fat?", you will get solutions. When you realize that eating is the way you cope with stress, you can learn to handle stress in a different way. "How" answers take you into Dr. Hills Slimming Plan. "Why" answers only give dead-end reasons which help you avoid listening to motivating "how" answers. The Goddess Phat only listens to you when you are very honest with yourself. She knows that what you need really is change. You can change if you will see the whole big problem as a series of smaller ones. If you think only of giant full-scale steps, you will automatically feel overwhelmed by your weight problem and you won't tackle it at all. Remember, you focus on success by concentrating on "how" solutions once you have your knowledge of how you are fat.

You can eat what you like on your free days, providing your choice does not have fat in it. Remember, most candy bars do have fats in them. On three alternate days you eat anything you like except things with fat, and the other four days of every week you shape up with Dr. Hills' diet aids. That's all the goddess demands of you. You will have the Galactomannan Nibblesticks and multivitamins and a number of other nutritious foods, and in addition you will have the most important ingredient—Spirulina—which makes the diet really work. Spirulina is critical to your success with the Slimming Plan.

Watch what happens as you begin to apply the principles of this plan. You will get self-respect as you get thin. Where does self-respect come from? It comes from setting a goal that is difficult but not impossible and then reaching it and setting another. Most dieters set impossible goals, and that is why they fail. Whereas before you used to swing between self-indulgence on the one hand and severity on the other, you now begin to realize that the severity never worked for very long and that this wasn't your fault. The fault was in the method itself. You don't need punishment; all you need is something that works. It may be something simple and ordinary, rather than something drastic and dramatic. The more you discover the slower steadier way, the more you will discover that every decrease of extremism gives you an increase of self-respect. Do not feel that you are once again in the position of trying to conquer your foe by the sheer force of will. The supplements offered in the Dr. Hills Slimming Plan will give you the edge you need while taking the edge *off* your hunger. You have already known the discouragement of a long, losing battle, but get ready; you are about to experience the excitement of winning!

Phat Traps

Because we carry it with us like a monkey on our back, *phattie* seems to be everywhere. Whenever we make one small mistake and fall into the monkey's hands, we decide we might as well give up for the rest of the day or week. In this way we undo months of effort and cut ourselves off from the Goddess of Slimming. Sometimes we can keep temptations to a minimum in our own house and protect ourselves from *phattie*, but no matter how carefully we structure our external environment, *phattie* can still tempt us from within until we have mastered that tempter.

When we go to restaurants, friends' houses, parties, etc., *phattie* is always there. Our host and hostess supply rich, tempting food and schedule the function or banquet at a different hour than our normal mealtime or on one of our shape up days. We have to be clever and switch our shape up day into a free day and by doing two shape up days in a row, enjoy the banquet. Always plan ahead. Think of the different kinds of temptations that will be placed before you and how you will respond. That way you will never be taken by surprise. Never arrive hungry. Listen to your goddess by taking your supplements one-half hour or even one hour before. *Phattie* always counts on your arriving hungry because *phattie* knows this weakens your defenses. If you're going to a dinner party in the evening of a free day, always eat your proper breakfast and lunch. If you are hungry before going to your party, fix yourself a nutritious snack or Spirulina shake before you go and take your Fiber-Lean and Spirulina with you if you have to. When *phattie* sees you walk into a party hungry, *phattie* goes straight for you. You can tell others you are on the Dr. Hills Slimming Plan and are devoted to the Goddess Phat. A sense of humor that can laugh about your fat helps you to let it go. *Phattie* loves it when people offer you the wrong foods because it knows that out of kindness you won't want to turn them down and you can then use the excuse, "They made me do it."

The restaurant is another of *phattie's* favorite hangouts. *Phattie* loves exotic restaurants where you can be tempted with lots of sauces and delicacies. While you can justify such extravagance on your free days, *phattie* can easily get you on one of your shape up days. Don't worry if you succumb, because that is just what *phattie* wants—for you to worry and feel bad. Just make sure you switch your free day with a balance day on which you take only Dr. Hills supplements.

The best way to beat *phattie* at this game, if you have to go to a restaurant, is to call ahead and have the staff prepare the kind of food you want without any fat content. Never look at a menu. Since you know what you want, ask for it, and ask for a salad immediately so that while you are waiting for the main course, *phattie* can't tempt you with bread, etc. Be the first to order so you can avoid the "me too" syndrome. For dessert, order fruits.

Dinner parties are another place *phattie* loves to hang out. If you are not on a slimming diet, then moderate alcohol is up to you, but for overweight people, alcohol turns to blood sugars and creates problems. If there is a bar at the party, head there immediately and order tomato juice or club soda. This way you will have something in your hand and no one will offer you a drink. One of the places *phattie* tries a sneak attack on you is in offering you too much alcohol. Another is fatty food and snack tables. Stay away from them by dancing or socializing. If it is your free day, you remind yourself that your Goddess of Slimming only allows you a stomach three-quarters full, the other one-quarter being needed for your health.

Famous *phattie* phrases:
* "You can take just one taste on your shape up day, can't you?"
* "I wish you'd eat on your shape up day so I won't have to feel alone."
* "You can have something extra on your shape up day, just this once."
* "It's a special occasion!"
* "One little bite won't hurt."
* "But I made it just for you!"

These inviting phrases are often innocent and they are spoken and backed up by special gestures of *phattie's* army— an outstretched hand offering a dish of candy on your free day; a warm smile across the cake plate; a careful set of eyes watching your response when a dish of goodies is passed around.

Do you have any of *phattie's* army in your life? Many of us do, perhaps a spouse, a parent, maybe a close friend who doesn't like our devotion to the Goddess of Slimming. Think back over the last couple of weeks—did someone offer you a fatty food you should not have had? Most people don't even realize they are working for *phattie*. They don't mean us any harm. They have the following rationalizations:

1. They know we don't really want to stay on our Slimming Plan and we feel deprived or lonely, so they will give us permission to eat, even though we already indulged ourself on our free day.

2. They are trying to be helpful because they feel overeating is good for us—after all, look at them, wanting to be indulgent.
3. They view offering food as a token of friendship and view refusal as a rejection of their friendship. The Goddess Phat tells them to invite you on your free day, not your balance day.
4. They may want to eat but feel they can't unless we join them. Or they may fear that if we change our shape we may change our friends and they'll lose us.

When someone offers you something fatty that is not good for you, refuse the offer in the name of the Goddess of Slimming (and mean it) while at the same time asking for something more nourishing. You are not a helpless victim in the hands of circumstances. The choice is always yours.

Some people believe they should be able to get *everything* they want. They want to eat and grow thin, and they do everything they can to have both. This is perfectly possible if they will eat Dr. Hills' satisfying diet aids and certain foods without fat in them and if they observe the rule—three-quarters full. But normally they are not satisfied and they stuff themselves, and the more they do, the fatter they grow until finally they have to take a hard cold look at reality. If dieters decide to master the desire for too much food and settle for just enough, they become tuned to a new aspect of themselves and begin to find joy. Dr. Hills' supplements give you a boost to mastery.

The skill of dieting lies in being neither too harsh with yourself nor too lenient. It may be better to be too drastic with *phattie* (who is really just the worst and lowest part of your own self) than to take no action at all. But there is also the danger of injuring both mind and body by a lack of compassion and respect for your being. Your Goddess of Slimming says, "Discipline yourself gently but firmly, and what you lose in weight, you will gain in character." Once you have conquered *phattie*, don't ever let weakness and negativity in again. Your success will gladden and inspire others to find the same fulfillment. *Phattie's* domain is the now. Eat now, pay later. At every moment, you have in your hands the power to create a new future. Once you decide to make war on *phattie*, you get very practical. When temptation presents itself, you are no longer its ally. You can keep your shape up days for the goddess.

Life is a Contest

It may be that the contest seems to be between you and your family or you and your friends or you and situations or even you and temptation, but the real contest is between two different parts of yourself. One part has a goal. It wants to gain back its self-respect. The other part wants short-term gratification at the expense of character and dignity. Everyone has a contest like this going on within them, though not everyone has it going on with food. To some people food is not even a temptation, and they may not be able to appreciate your struggle to gain mastery in that area, but they may themselves be wrestling with some other thing that for you is easy. It is always easy to master the other fellow's problem. Have you ever heard the expression, "My something is your nothing"?

But never mind the other fellow. If you look just at yourself, you will be ready to end the contest once and for all, ready to put out enough energy so you will reach your long-range goal, even if it means that you have to find some ways of dealing with the short-term impulses. Food is something that is coming into you from outside, but now we are talking about something that goes *out* of you from *inside*. That something is your spirit. Do not underestimate its power! If you use the diet supplements in this Slimming Plan to help you deal with hunger, your spirit can do the rest. You will be amazed at how strong it actually is and how good it feels when it begins to win the contest.

REMEMBER

* Your mind has the power to make or break your attempt to lose weight.

* Misguided attitudes and beliefs can destroy all your efforts, no matter how sincerely you intend to succeed.

* Look at your normal habits of eating and of dieting; consciously avoid them as you create entirely new ways of dealing with your weight.

* One part of you will try to tempt you into weakness, doubt, discouragement, uncertainty, rationalization, and self-destruction.

* Another part of you is strong and clear-minded and certain of its direction; this part is slow and steady, rather than severe and hasty.

* The secret of losing weight is to stop believing you are at the mercy of the negative side of yourself and trapped in its emotions.

* You can consciously shift over to the strong part of yourself, once you realize that the weak part is not really you but is your *enemy*.

* The slow, steady way brings self-respect.

* You need not be dependent on going hungry or having to rely on will power alone; you have Spirulina and Fiber-Lean and other supplements to help you, and you can enjoy eating without any guilt whatsoever on your "free days".

* Once you give your spirit a fair chance at self-mastery without the undue pressure of hunger, you will find that your spirit is incredibly strong.

EXERCISE MEANS ENERGY

Exercise is the key which most diets mention but really ignore. There is no excuse not to exercise, but how do you get the will to do it? To an overweight person, exercise is like running uphill with a backpack full of heavy Coke bottles. Slim, trim athletic people feel so peppy that they want to share their good fortune. They say, "You just need to run a couple of miles each day; it'll make you feel great." But the only time you tried it, you probably felt terrible. So what is the answer? One answer is Spirulina, which may alter your production of energy. Another answer is to start where you are, not where others are, and not where you *wish* you were. If you haven't moved out of your chair in the last twenty years, your first step is to move out of it. If you are used to walking a block a day, increase it to two. Later you can increase it to three and then four, and so on, but not right away. Fanatics are extremists. They starve themselves one week and then gorge the next, or they exercise so vigorously that they end up in bed, immobile for the next two weeks. But no fanatic really knows how to lose weight, because what it requires is slow, steady persistence and patience. So you must choose a kind of exercise you will want to persist in, not one that you hate and must force yourself to do. Some people can dance all night and not even think of it as exercise. Others like to dig in the garden. Find the kind of movement you enjoy and you will do it as often as you can.

EXERCISE IS TO THE BODY WHAT FOOD IS TO YOU. DO NOT STARVE IT.

Surplus energy in the body is not something you spend or save. A body does not need to wear out as it gets older. Instead, the human body repairs itself with exercise and improves itself with use. Proper exercise not only improves physical fitness but reduces weight. It is well known by medical doctors that exercise reduces the risks of heart disease and increases the flexibility of all the organs of the body.

Most people just jump right into activity without preparing their bodies for it. This can be especially shocking to your body if it happens to be overweight or if you are not used to exercising. If you force your body or overexert, neither Dr. Hills nor the Light Force Company will be answerable for it. You should see your doctor if you are going to do something strenuous or if you have been under a doctor's care. All exercise should be appropriate to an individual's age and general physical condition. People of any age can exercise by walking and swimming, bending and walking up stairways.

Exercise does not have to be a chore; it can be recreation. To take a walk with a friend is very different from making yourself walk to lose weight. You can make exercise one of your favorite forms of recreation and pleasure. Instead of sitting in a dark movie house or even going for a drive in a car, you can walk, swim or play tennis.

Decrease Your Weight
By Spending Energy

Regardless of whether you are counting calories or not, your body will need to metabolize more calories than you consume each day in order to lose weight. The following chart is given, not to get you into counting but to let you see which activities will bring you the best results in losing weight.

Activity	Number of Calories Lost Per Hour
Lying down or sleeping	80
Sitting	100
Standing	130
Walking at a leisurely pace, approximately 2 miles/hr.	210
Driving your car	120
Bicycling	210
Domestic work	180
Lawnmowing, by a handmower	270
Lawnmowing, by a powermower	250
Woodchopping or sawing	400
Golf	250
Bowling	270
Swimming	300
Roller skating	350
Ping-Pong	360
Tennis	420
Waterskiing	480
Hill-climbing	490
Running	900
Skiing	600
Ice-skating	400
Volleyball	350
Handball and squash	600
Dancing	240
Climbing Stairs	1200

If you eat little and move little, you will still put on weight, and if you want to eat cake, you may as well forget the calories you will lose by jogging or running. If you want to keep the effects of your jogging and make them long-lasting, you don't eat or do things that make you have to run around the block for four hours just to lose a regained pound of fat. Forget about your previous failures at dieting and begin a program of mental and physical activity *every day*.

A marathon runner never gets fat but needs many calories of energy, while a fat person needs only enough calories to keep the cells functioning and the process of protein and fat metabolism going. Therefore fat people need exercise more than anyone else. Lack of exercise not only causes fat to pile up as unused energy but also causes a certain kind of fat to accumulate which some call cellulite.

The Truth About Cellulite

Cellulite is a concept put forward by beauty experts which refers to the lumps and bulges of "orange peel" fat. Cellulite is supposed to be fat which is trapped in connective tissues and saturated with water and waste. These experts believe that these pockets of "fat gone wrong" act like sponges that absorb water, blow up and bulge out, resulting in flabby ripples, and that a low-calorie diet is no solution to the problem. They say that such a diet reduces fat, but that the cellulite ripples will remain. In order to remove this fat, they recommend diets with low-fat foods, fruits and vegetables, yogurt, low salt and plenty of water. They also recommend exercise, massage, relaxation, deep breathing and overworking the kidneys and sweat glands in saunas, and consuming lots of natural laxatives to overwork the intestines.

The Dr. Hills Slimming Plan regards cellulite as just plain fat. Fat differs from one human being to another. The latest thinking is that there are two kinds of fat-holding tissues: one that holds fat for quick conversion into energy and another that holds fat for slower conversion into reserve energy. The "orange peel" fat called cellulite appears on inactive people and can also appear on people who are not even fat and who have dieted all their life. However, cellulite rarely appears on active people who take regular exercise. Cellulite, then, is just plain fat which accumulates near the surface of the skin and is a product of the sedentary life. Massage alone will not remove it. All the dietary recommendations of the cellulite diets are good, especially the good elimination, which is essential in keeping the body fluids down, since too much fluid contributes to the "orange peel" effect. But the real key is *exercise*, which is recommended by the Dr. Hills Slimming Plan.

How Does Good Digestion Affect Weight Loss and How Does Exercise Affect Digestion?

The stomach hydrolizes proteins, that is, steeps your food in hydrochloric acid which dissolves the protein into its basic amino acid contents. To do this effectively it must churn the food and, although you cannot feel it, the muscles of the stomach constantly push the chewed food around to expose it to the gastric juices. If there is not enough room for the stomach to churn, its muscles become slack and the food sits there undigested like a lead weight and is only half digested. Improper digestion means you lose the food value of some important amino acids your cells need for proper fat metabolism. Most of the calories in proteins are used for metabolism of cell proteins and do a different job than fats and carbohydrates. Bad protein digestion means your health deteriorates and then food becomes toxic waste. Exercise helps the muscles to keep their tone and churn your food.

When the fats and carbohydrates pass through the acid churning of the stomach, they are then passed on into the intestines where they are broken down. If the muscles in the walls of the intestine are sluggish and cannot push the food along, they will lose their muscle tone and leave the food clogged in the intestinal tube. Exercise helps the peristaltic action of the muscles to move it along and the strange thing is, if you are clogged up with toxic wastes you never feel the energy to exercise and you constantly feel a dull headache or feel no zest for life. Exercise and proper digestion in the alimentary system are like putting oil in your car; it helps the system to work so it can burn the fuel easier and makes all the parts work. If your parts get stuck and won't work, no amount of good nutrition, vitamins or expensive food can help you to lose weight because a clogged stomach and intestine, clogged through overfilling and lack of exercise, is like a car whose carburetor has been flooded with too much fuel. Not much exercise is needed for a healthy system, but a sedentary life without activity leads to a more sedentary and sluggish system.

As you exercise, your body is converting stored glycogen into energy. Instead of thinking that you wish you were doing something else instead of exercising, think about the way the body metabolizes its energy. First the cells must get nutrients from your bloodstream, but they cannot do so if your circulation is sluggish or your capillaries do not carry the nutrients to the site where they are needed. The cells metabolize fats and carbohydrates through a process called oxidation. We use oxygen by carrying it along in the blood and burning it with other nutrients for energy. We excrete carbon dioxide as a waste product by breathing it out of our lungs. If we need more energy than is supplied by the fuel we have eaten, the liver starts to break down its stored glycogen which helps to release more oxygen. The thing to realize is that the cells of our bodies are breathing in oxygen and excreting carbon dioxide just as we are. Think of these cells taking in the nutrients and elements they need and excreting what they don't need, so that they can keep you supplied with energy; think of them burning the stored glycogen when you have not supplied them with food as an excess of fuel; think of them storing more and more fuel, when you have supplied too much food.

Glycogen stores up your excess energy in starch for quick use later in exercise, running or activity. It is your first call on your reserves of energy. When there is still more surplus, the oxygen which would have been burned up in activity is then stored as fat for long-term energy reserve. Therefore if you don't use or burn up the energy you get from food, you must get fat. Intense brain activity uses just as much energy/oxygen as the body does, so people who make mental efforts also remain thin if they consume more oxygen than they store up. But even these mentally active people need some physical exercise not only to burn off the surplus fat but to strengthen the muscles of the stomach and digestive tract.

REMEMBER

* You may feel that you have too little energy to waste any of it on exercise, but if you exercise, you will have *more* energy, not less!

* You need exercise to lose weight; you need it even if you don't want to lose weight.

* To deny your body exercise because you don't like it or feel too busy is to be unkind to a part of *yourself*. Have compassion and do not deny your body's needs.

* The secret is not to think of it as "exercise" (a thing we *should* do) but as doing something we want and like to do.

FINDING WHAT WORKS

The products recommended in the Dr. Hills Slimming Plan are not only pure and natural, they are effective. To buy a product that is pure does not always mean it will do anything for you. The Light Force Company puts all its effort into producing products that will work. This is how it has become such a flourishing company in the short time since it was founded in December 1979. From the outset, its motto was to give its customers only those products which would help them build physical and spiritual health and well-being. At first it seemed like it might take years to introduce a completely new food—Spirulina—to the American public and educate people about its value, but instead, the product became an almost overnight success. People didn't care if it was an algae or *what* it was, because it worked! Then came OB-1, with the same instantaneous acclaim. And each new product thereafter has been well received, simply because people can feel a difference. The best way to do business is to care about people. Then they respond naturally, and there is no need for the extra selling manipulations of professional advertising or any other tactics. Sincerity, integrity, and caring have produced these products for the Dr. Hills Slimming Plan:

Spirulina
Fiber-Lean
Ram Bam Bread
Galactomannan Nibblesticks
Omega Boost One
Lecithin[Plus]

Bee Sweet Pollen
Tienchi Boost
ZMS Boost
Garlic Spirulina
Manna Powder
Green Gold
Wildfire

Light Force 100% Spirulina

Spirulina is low in calories but amazingly high in nutrition your body craves, with fourteen minerals and nine important vitamins. Its nourishing and compact protein contains eighteen amino acids—the body's building blocks—and *all eight essential amino acids*. These amino acids are rarely found in vegetable sources in the correct proportion, but Spirulina's 70% protein gives your hard-working body sustaining energy to last all day. This 70% protein is up to 95% digestible protein as compared with beef's 20%. And because it is complete and easily digestible protein, much less Spirulina is needed to meet the recommended daily protein allowance than you would need of foods which have other qualities of protein.

Gram for gram, this delicious plankton contains 20 times the protein and about the same calcium as milk and about 2.64 times the protein of dried whole milk. It contains 350% more potassium than rice, and 300% more iron than steak! Spirulina provides the essential B vitamins, which work together as a family, and is a wonderfully potent source of Vitamin B-12. Liver, a fat-laden meat, was once thought to be the most concentrated source of this important vitamin, but scientific tests prove that Spirulina contains 250% more B-12 than an equal amount of liver.

Spirulina is endowed with an abundance of biological pigments such as beta carotene which the body uses to produce its own Vitamin A. One serving of Spirulina powder supplies 600% of the USRDA for Vitamin A, but because the body converts beta carotene to A *only as needed*, there is no threat of toxic buildup of Vitamin A. Phycocyanin is another biliprotein pigment in Spirulina, containing large amounts of cobalamin derived from cobalt.

Rare carbohydrates in the Spirulina are an energy bonus, such as rhamnose, a sugar absorbed by the blood, which is quickly made available to your muscles, and glycogen—a starch stored in our livers as reserve energy. Glycogen is found in no other plant life on the planet but blue-green algae like Spirulina.

Fasting With Spirulina

Concentrated and nutrient-packed Spirulina is an excellent source of sustaining energy while fasting. Very little protein is stored in the human body, so fasting can quickly deplete these important reserves. If your body does not receive the protein it needs to build and maintain tissues, it will break down less important structures to free the amino acids necessary to build more vital tissues. Internally this depletion can result in a lack of blood protein, enzymes, antibodies and hormones and externally can be seen in newly-appearing wrinkles and inadequate muscle tone. Spirulina mixed in juice can supply your protein needs and help you avoid these potential problems while you are cleansing your system.

Fiber-Lean

Fiber-Lean is an amazing new galactomannan soy product from Europe which works in natural harmony with your

TYPICAL CHEMICAL ANALYSIS OF SPIRULINA

(Analysis done by TNO, a government-sponsored, UN-approved laboratory.)

CHEMICAL COMPOSITION

Moisture	7.0%
Ash	9.0%
Proteins	60-71.0%
Crude fiber	0.9%
Xanthophylls	1.80 g/kg of product
Carotene	1.90 g/kg of product
Chlorophyll a	7.60 g/kg of product

TOTAL ORGANIC NITROGEN   13.35%

Nitrogen from Proteins	11.36%
Crude Protein (%N x 6.25)	60-71.0%

ESSENTIAL AMINOACIDS

Isoleucine	4.13%
Leucine	5.80%
Lysine	4.00%
Methionine	2.17%
Phenylalanine	3.95%
Threonine	4.17%
Tryptophan	1.13%
Valine	6.00%

NON-ESSENTIAL AMINOACIDS

Alanine	5.82%
Arginine	5.98%
Aspartic Acid	6.43%
Cystine	0.67%
Glutamic Acid	8.94%
Glycine	3.46%
Histidine	1.08%
Proline	2.97%
Serine	4.00%
Tyrosine	4.60%

VITAMINS

Biotin (H)	average	0.4	mg/kg
Cyanocobalamin (B_{12})	average	2	mg/kg
d-Ca-Pantothenate	average	11	mg/kg
Folic Acid	average	0.5	mg/kg
Inositol	average	350	mg/kg
Nicotinic Acid (PP)	average	118	mg/kg
Pyridoxine (B_6)	average	3	mg/kg
Riboflavine (B_2)	average	40	mg/kg
Thiamine (B_1)	average	55	mg/kg
Tocopherol (E)	average	190	mg/kg

MOISTURE	7.0%
ASH	9.0%

Calcium (Ca)	1,315 mg/kg
Phosphorus (P)	8,942 mg/kg
Iron (Fe)	580 mg/kg
Sodium (Na)	412 mg/kg
Chloride (Cl)	4,400 mg/kg
Magnesium (Mg)	1,915 mg/kg
Manganese (Mn)	25 mg/kg
Zinc (Zn)	39 mg/kg
Potassium (K)	15,400 mg/kg
Others	57,000 mg/kg

STEROLS	
Cholesterol	325 mg/kg
Sitosterol	196 mg/kg
	97 mg/kg

Dihidro 7 Cholesterol Cholesten 7 ol 3 Stigmasterol others	— 32 mg/kg

NUTRITIONAL VALUE

Protein Efficiency Ratio (PER) of 2.2 to 2.6 (74-87% that of casein)
Net Protein Utilization (NPU) of 53 to 61% (85-92% that of casein)
Digestibility of 83 to 84%

Available Lysine	average	85%
NITROGEN FROM NUCLEIC ACIDS		1.99%
Ribonucleic Acid (RNA) RNA = N × 2.18		3.50%
Deoxyribonucleic Acid (DNA) DNA = N × 2.63		1.00%

CAROTENOIDS		4,000	mg/kg

α Carotene		traces	
β Carotene	average	1,700	mg/kg
Xanthophylis	average	1,000	mg/kg
Cryptoxanthin	average	556	mg/kg
Echinenone	average	439	mg/kg
Zeaxanthin	average	316	mg/kg
Lutein and Euglenanone	average	289	mg/kg

TOTAL LIPIDS		7.0%
Fatty Acids		5.7%
Lauric (C_{12})		229 mg/kg
Myristic (C_{14})		644 mg/kg
Palmitic (C_{16})		21,141 mg/kg
Palmitoleic (C_{16})		2,035 mg/kg
Palmitolinoleic (C_{16})		2,565 mg/kg
Heptadecanoic (C_{17})		142 mg/kg
Stearic (C_{18})		353 mg/kg
Oleic (C_{18})		3,009 mg/kg
Linoleic (C_{18})		13,784 mg/kg
γ Linolenic (C_{18})		11,970 mg/kg
α Linolenic (C_{18})		427 mg/kg
Others		699 mg/kg
Insaponifiable		1.3%
Sterols		325 mg/kg
Titerpen alcohols		800 mg/kg
Carotenoids		4,000 mg/kg
Chlorophyll a		7,600 mg/kg
Others		150 mg/kg
3-4 Benzypyrene		3.6 mg/kg

TOTAL CARBOHYDRATES		16.5%
Rhamnose	average	9.0%
Glucane	average	1.5%
Phosphoryled cyclitols	average	2.5%
Glucosamine and muramic acid	average	2.0%
Glycogen	average	0.5%
Sialic acid and others	average	0.5%

Editor's Note: In all laboratory tests of Spirulina, there will be differences in each test, each sample and each laboratory because Spirulina is a natural product varying in pigments, proteins and carbohydrates with the seasons and local conditions. This analysis was done by a Dutch laboratory on behalf of the United Nations.

body to help you lose weight. Extensive use in Germany indicates that Fiber-Lean helps the obese lose weight quickly, safely and effectively.

Unusually nutritious Fiber-Lean is up to 60% protein and 40% carbohydrate. Protein provides you with sustaining energy throughout the day, resulting in a more constant blood sugar level. Twenty five percent of the carbohydrate is galactomannan fiber and 25% is arabinomannan and the rest are nutritional polysaccharides which also give energy. Often, when you are dieting, blood sugar levels rise and fall, and you must endure the accompanying "highs and lows". Israeli research has shown that by supplying the body with a combination of protein and fiber, people experience a more constant blood sugar level. The galactomannan fiber also provides valuable roughage and bulk for a sensation of fullness.

There is scientific evidence that fiber may lower blood cholesterol levels in the body, possibly through aiding in the rapid elimination of cholesterol-rich foods from the intestines. While there are many types of fiber, not all help the body in this way. Studies on wheat bran prove it to be inconsistent in reducing cholesterol.

To date, Fiber-Lean is the most nutritious fiber product on the market and the only one that is proven clinically by Israel's most prestigious institution to aid dieters. Rambam Hospital in Israel puts 25% of Fiber-Lean in their regular bread. Dr. Hills Fiber-Lean can be eaten "as is" or mixed with water, milk, yogurt, soups, or juices of any kind. It can be added to baked goods, meat loaves, cereals and other foods. You will find it a pleasant-tasting, easy-to-use, nutritious source of galactomannan fiber for people dieting, fasting, or simply wanting more roughage for regularity. It is also relatively free of natural sugars, starches and fat and contains no artificial chemicals, additives, sweeteners or preservatives.

Fiber-Lean is an extract from the cotyledon of the soybean hull, but all the antinutrients usually present in the soybean cotyledon hulls have been removed by a special patented process to create Fiber-Lean, whereas all other diet fibers on the U.S. market derived from soybean hulls contain (at this time of writing) these adverse antinutritional factors. The big companies know this and therefore do not use this fiber but turn to less nutritional fibers. But the small companies take the risk of leaving the antinutrients in. Hence Fiber-Lean is a unique product because of this special extraction process which removes harmful saponins and other components of soy, including enzyme inhibitors. The process enhances the galactomannan and arabinomannan fibers which are nutritionally superior to glucomannan, starch blockers, etc. Fiber-Lean is:

> 40–60% protein
> 30–50% fiber (including arabinomannan fibers)
> 5% minerals
> high in potassium (2%)
> low in sodium (0.01%)

Its fibers are made of special sugars:

> 25% pectic like acidic polysaccharides
> 25% of the carbohydrate is galactomannans
> 25% of the carbohydrate is arabinomannans
> 25% consists of other complex mannans

The fact that Fiber-Lean is high in polysaccharide fibers means that you get energy but with low calories.

Before You Begin With Fiber-Lean

If you take too little liquid, you may experience a temporary problem with constipation, since Fiber-Lean absorbs many times its weight in moisture. In fact, this absorption of liquid is the source of its remarkable cleansing action. When taken with water or juices, the galactomannans fibers swell up inside the intestine and are not attacked by the hydrochloric acid in the normal stomach. You must begin to adapt your stomach little by little to the "full feeling" of the fiber by starting with one teaspoonful, one-half hour before meals, gradually increasing up to one or two tablespoonfuls as desired. You can take more than one tablespoon before each meal; the Rambam Hospital uses two tablespoons as part of its regular program. But I have found this does not feel so comfortable at the beginning, so it is best to begin with smaller amounts and work up to higher amounts over a two-week period. The action of the bowel is different with each individual person.

Once your stomach and intestine get used to the swelling of these fibers, the fiber products will regularize the bowel movements and help to satiate your hunger feelings so you will eat smaller amounts of food. Once you get regular and let the galactomannan fiber do the dieting for you, you will find your own level. You can actually take up to eighteen teaspoonfuls a day, but you should find what works best for you. Until you get used to it, taking small amounts will not cause any blockages and will actually soften the feces and help to expel it quicker.

Ram Bam Bread

This delicious bread is wonderful for weight loss. You can enjoy eating bread in the Dr. Hills Slimming Plan like you've never enjoyed bread before when trying to lose weight, because you know that the fiber is good for slimming. Since Ram Bam Bread has a high level of protein and a very high level of nondigestible polysaccharides, it contributes to a feeling of fullness, thus causing one to eat less. Once the body is used to the fiber, the product will help regulate normal bowel activity. Once you have tried these little brown buns, you will find Ram Bam Bread one of your favorites in the Dr.

Hills Slimming Plan. Eat Rambam Hospital's delicious bread only on your free days.

Galactomannan Nibblesticks

These tasty bread sticks are ideal for parties or for midday snacks. They are crunchy and delicious and supply you with high-protein fiber for slimming while making you feel as though you have had a treat. These are also excellent to satisfy hunger on your shape up days.

Omega Boost One

Omega Boost One (OB-1), which earned its name for its complete formula, is created from the finest sources available and meets the USRDA for every essential vitamin and mineral. Your body uses these important nutrients to burn stored fat. OB-1 is thus your dieting insurance which also helps you get the most out of all the foods you do eat. It also gives you all the vitamins you need during your fasting periods.

OB-1's sustained release "portions out" nutrients gradually, supplying 100% or more of the following: Vitamins A, D, C, B-1, B-2, B-6, B-12, E, niacin, pantothenic acid, folic acid, biotin, calcium, magnesium, iodine, copper, zinc and many trace elements for which no RDAs have been set.

OB-1 contains all natural ingredients wherever possible and is boosted with the extra nutrition of Spirulina, wheatgrass, bee pollen, garlic, tienchi and red ginsengs, Mineral 72, and bioflavonoids. There is no higher multivitamin on the market, and comparison of other vitamin labels with this all-in-one daily supplement shows this to be a fact. We are told by the largest custom tableting operation in the business that ours is the top among more than 300 manufacturers who supply the trade.

Lecithin^Plus

Lecithin^Plus is a delicious blend of 100% soy lecithin and Spirulina boosted with Vitamins A, C, B-6 and yeast, which is naturally abundant with 17 vitamins. Brimming with the nutrients so essential to health, Lecithin^Plus is a vital ingredient to this diet and a super addition to smoothies.

Lecithin helps emulsify fat and fat-soluble nutrients—such as Vitamins A, E, and D—thus allowing your body to receive these necessary elements. Lecithin accounts for 30 to 40% of the brain's weight and is found in especially high concentrations in the liver and heart, also. Generally nutritionists agree that if the body has insufficient amounts of lecithin, blood cholesterol levels may rise. There is some evidence that lecithin may also help reduce the size of cholesterol particles so they do not become lodged in arterial walls.

Lecithin is made up of several parts, two of which are the B vitamins inositol and choline. These vitamins work together to assist brain function and aid in memory. It is thought that inositol may assist in the redistribution of body fat, as well.

Bee Sweet™ Pollen

One teaspoon of precious Bee Sweet™ Pollen contains 2,500,000,000 grains of plant pollen and represents 600 working bee hours! It's no wonder that this "ambrosia of the gods" packs a nutritional punch. Pollen, the male germ seed of flowers, is the "survival food" of the hive, and countless cultures throughout the centuries have recognized its value. A staple food of the ancient Greek and Roman athletes, pollen has long been revered by those seeking perfect health and stamina.

Science reveals the incredible wealth of nutrients found in this delicious golden food: 20 of the 22 amino acids required by humans are contained in bee pollen, along with 16 vitamins, 16 minerals, 18 enzymes and 28 other assorted elements such as nucleic acids, RNA and DNA, fructose and glucose. Bee pollen is over 25% protein and 15% lecithin, a compound comprising 30 to 40% of the brain's weight.

This low-calorie, sweet treat encourages balanced vitality and boosts energy levels as it supplies all the nutrients your body needs to burn fat away.

Tienchi Boost

Ginseng is an ancient herb, well known throughout the world for its restorative powers. In China it is used to rejuvenate and purify. The legendary ginseng root is highly prized in China for its potent herbal properties. Extensive scientific research into glycosides has recently revealed the fact behind the legend: special nutrients in ginseng (saponins) go directly into the bloodstream and help carry other important elements to your body's cells. This encourages greater biological activity in the cells, thereby promoting health and vitality. In the U.S.A. we are unable to promote the medical research which the Chinese government doctors openly discuss in their publications.

Of all the ginsengs, tienchi is the most revered. In China it is called the "King of Ginsengs" for its superior qualities. Taking approximately 7 years to mature, tienchi ginseng is sold in Hong Kong for high prices. Tienchi Boost is made of the best ginseng money can buy to help spark the zest and energy which will enhance any dieter's ability to succeed!

ZMS Boost

Chelated zinc is important for your mental and physical well-being and gives you the power to metabolize efficiently. ZMS Boost actually contains three important minerals all in one tablet to stimulate your body into health and energy.

Zinc

Zinc is a little dynamo because at least 90 enzymes require the presence of zinc in order to make your system function properly. These enzymes are vital to your body because their metabolic reactions help you to burn off surplus fat.

You also need zinc for production of insulin which is a hormone you secrete to deal with blood sugar levels. If your blood sugars are not balanced and you go on a diet you will get "highs and lows" which will affect your ability to resist the desire for sweets and other fattening delectables. You want to avoid cravings caused by these ups and downs.

Molybdenum

Your red blood cells which transport oxygen to every cell in your body need this wonderful mineral. No RDA has been set for it, but it forms part of an enzyme which collects potentially harmful nitrogen compounds released during the digestion of proteins. Soils are deprived of molybdenum in certain areas which make it important for you to put it back into your food intake.

Selenium

Selenium works with other vitamins like Vitamin E to produce antibodies but also does a special job in controlling an enzyme called glutathione peroxidase which regulates free radicals which float around in your body and attach themselves to various kinds of fat.

Fat in your body, especially the kind of fat which we call unsaturated fat, attracts to itself the oxygen molecule. When the oxygen joins together with fats, your body tends to make water and lipid peroxides. These peroxides are left over in your body after the water has been made from the fat molecule so it's not good to keep them roving freely around your body until the peroxidase can kill them off. Vitamin E working with selenium protects against these disintegrations of unsaturated fats by working as an antioxidant. So oxygen molecules are prevented from linking up with your fat and you can then get rid of your fat by using it up properly. The Slimming Plan does the rest, but it's good to know why you should not eat more fatty foods.

NOTE: as these three ingredients are trace minerals and they are only needed by the body in trace amounts, do not make the mistake of thinking "if a little is good, more must be better". Take only the amount recommended. More will probably do more harm than good. I have already tested these quantities out with many people, so be sure to follow instructions.

Garlic Spirulina

Garlic Spirulina is a potent blend of garlic and parsley—two natural herbs long valued for their cleansing properties—boosted with Spirulina. Today garlic and parsley are important for their high vitamin and mineral content as well as their versatile uses in foods and teas which appear to soothe and help cleanse the body.

Cleansing your body from the inside out is the first step in changing its shape and vitality. Providing your body with wholesome foods such as Spirulina, gives it the opportunity to form strong tissues from natural elements. As a consequence, the body can begin to replace the toxins, which have been stored over the years, with healthier nutrients.

Manna Powder

For your protein-powered body we have created Manna Powder, a combination of three complete proteins: Spirulina, soybeans isolated to 90% protein, and yeast fortified with spinach, peas and the essential amino acid methionine.

Manna Powder is a convenient and low-calorie protein "punch" to add to smoothies, juice, soups or salads without the fats, hormones and preservatives often found in animal products. Protein amino acids, the essential building blocks of your body, are used daily to build and maintain all tissues and organs. In fact, one-third of the 70 trillion cells which make up your body are constantly aging, wearing out and being replaced. Good quality protein is vital to this maintenance process as well as to your natural defense system and for forming hormones and enzymes.

Manna Powder is also high in the B complex vitamins, which are so important for the proper assimilation of food, and in phosphorus, a mineral necessary to nerve functions, heart regularity and bone formation.

Manna Powder is a delicious, nutritious treat to help speed you to your low-calorie replacement meal whenever you are feeling hungry. It can be mixed with delicious flavors, as milkshakes and in your favorite fruit juices.

Green Gold

This special blend of Spirulina, bee pollen, ginseng and papaya enzyme deserves its name, for its vitalizing fuel packs a potent punch. Spirulina and bee pollen, two complete proteins, give an invigorating boost with low calories. And the addition of papaya enzyme aids the digestion of these amino acids. (The natural enzymes from papaya are important, for they break down fats as well as protein.) The unique glycosides and sugars in ginseng—the most revered herb in Chinese medicine—go directly into the blood and help carry other nutrients to your cells. These, along with the natural sugars and pigments in Spirulina and the predigested sugars in bee pollen, promote biological activity in your cells . . . helping to provide a feeling of youthful energy.

Wildfire

Wildfire is a natural choice for dieters! In this product, Spirulina—already rich in B vitamins—is enhanced with Vitamins B-6 and niacin. Together these nutrients work to aid the functioning of the brain and central nervous system, the production of red blood cells, and the metabolism of proteins, fats and carbohydrates. Generally, the B vitamins are responsible for sparking metabolic reactions, such as converting the food you eat into nutrients the body can assimilate or helping to metabolize stored fat.

In particular, niacin aids circulation—a vital function which helps to distribute nutrients and oxygen to the cells and eliminate wastes. Some people get a warm flushed feeling called a "niacin rush". If this feeling is uncomfortable you will want to take only one Wildfire instead of two. Vitamin B-6 is especially important for the metabolism of protein; should you lack this vitamin, your body cannot absorb amino acids.

One of the most amazing benefits of Wildfire is its combination of Spirulina and calcium gluconate. These naturally combine in your stomach to create pangamic acid—the so-called "B-15". Many runners report quicker "recovery times" when taking Wildfire, and we know you'll love the burst of B vitamins and benefits that Wildfire supplies.

Optional Products

In addition to the products which are essential to the Dr. Hills Slimming Plan, there are certain optional products which you can also take to gain good health and renewal of the life force. These may not be within everyone's budget, but for those who treasure health more than cigarettes or will spend money on vital nutrition instead of alcohol or movies, I would recommend these optional products.

Special Ginseng (optional)

This unique product combines a superb blend of ginsengs —including the highly sought tienchi—with naturally potent bee pollen. These ginsengs contain glycosides, the sugars which have been shown to help fight fatigue in laboratory test animals. The invigorating properties of tienchi complement the relaxing attributes of the Chinese and American ginsengs (*Acanthopanax* and *Panax Red* Ginsengs and *Panax Quinque folium*). All work together with high potency bee pollen (chock full of special sugars and nutrients) to promote greater biological activity in the cells. SPECIAL GINSENG is an invigorating pick-me-up to encourage your body to natural zest!

For weight watchers, ginseng gives the great feeling of well-being expected by eating rich foods.

Life Force (optional)

Life Force may be the sustained energy our body is craving. Life Force combines Spirulina with English Brewer's yeast in a product designed to help fight stress and provide energy.

Carbohydrates and protein work together to help keep your blood sugar levels stable. Spirulina and yeast are superior fuels for your body because they supply complete proteins for sustained, gradual energy release; supplying a balanced release, helping blood sugar levels stabilize and combating the erratic highs and lows often associated with cutting back on calories.

Yeast and Spirulina are low in sugar, starch and fat, so it is their high quality proteins which satiate your body, while helping to deliver the "pep" you need to succeed with a reduced calorie program.

A Cornucopia of Vitamins

In addition to its high protein content, yeast contains an abundance of vitamins—ten in all, including these well known ones: B-1, B-2, B-3, B-6, pantothenic acid, folic acid, inositol, choline, and PABA.

Spirulina is the highest known source of Vitamin B-12, and it complements yeast's vitamin profile with carotenes, the precursors for Vitamin A. This fat-soluble vitamin can pose a threat if too much is ingested at once, for it is stored in the tissues. Because carotenes are only converted to Vitamin A as needed by the body, there is no threat of a toxic build-up.

The B complex vitamins, including folic acid, inositol and choline work as a team to provide many benefits to your body. They are vitally important to the body's reaction to stress, and are essential parts of enzymatic structures which convert food into the fuel your body burns.

Jolli-Tea (optional)

For thousands of years, even before recorded history, people have harvested wild herbs to strengthen healthy metabolisms and spark vitality. Dr. Hills Jolli-Tea is a unique blend of thirteen herbs that will keep you awake and alive and give you a light-hearted lift. Replace the harsh acidity of coffee or tea with this rousing blend whenever you need a quick pick-me-up. Whether you are working, studying, or playing, you will need sharp awareness, elevated mood, or stamina. Turn to Jolli-Tea instead of to a cookie to perk you up.

When Dr. Hills visited Kenya and Ethiopia, he found large groups of people going without food for days. They were active, with plenty of energy, and were not hungry. These people shared that their lack of hunger was due to many of the same herbs found in Jolli-Tea's unique blend.

Jolli-Tea will keep you wide awake, so don't take it just before bedtime. Give two capsules to truck drivers who drive at night. Jolli-Tea is used by slimmers to keep the mood and energy up and up. This natural product includes herbs also used in folklore for cleansing and invigorating the body.

The ingredients of JOLLI-TEA are: ephedra bush, acanthopanax senticosus, red ginseng, damiana, kava-kava, ginger root, fo-ti, gentian root, hawthorne berries, dong quai, cassia tora, golden seal, black pepper.

Mineral 72 (optional)

Minerals perform two vital functions in your body: they are important components of enzymes—the proteins which convert the food you eat into nutrients the body uses for energy—and they perform as structures within cells, such as calcium within bone cells.

When rocks weather and decompose, they lose minerals to the surrounding environment. Rains wash the minerals into rivers, over the land and into the sea. Plants and algae take them up, converting them to chelated (bonded) nutrients on which we rely. Today, however, many soils are minerally depleted due to modern farming methods. Fruits and vegetables, which depend on the soil and water for these elements, are therefore deficient as well. In addition, many of our modern foods are stripped of their mineral content during processing. If you are concerned about getting all the essential minerals your body needs, supplements can offer *nutrient insurance.*

The unique and wonderful aspect of Mineral 72 is that it contains over 72 major minerals and trace minerals in chelated form because they are taken from a sea deposit of ancient kelp beds. Mineral 72 helps your body get the most from the foods you eat by supplying you with a natural abundance of nutrients for health. The minerals which trigger the production of enzymes help to activate all bodily functions, including the metabolic process which converts body fat to energy!

Silica 47% (optional)

Silica 47% is a rich clay substance, the result of ancient geological activity, high in the valuable mineral silica and other important elements. Next to oxygen, silicon is the most abundant element on earth, making up to one-quarter of the earth's crust. Silica does not occur alone but is found in combination with other elements in the form of silicon or silicates. Just as silica forms an integral part of the earth's structure so it is also an essential component of human hair, nails, teeth and connective tissue, which binds cells together —giving them shape and strength. Researchers believe silicon may play a vital role in keeping connective tissues—

such as cartilage, tendons and blood vessels (including the heart aorta)—strong and resilient.

Scientists have recently discovered that many minerals work together with vitamins to perform the multitude of maintenance tasks required each day in you: body. It is becoming increasingly clear that no element functions alone, and many trace minerals previously thought to be unnecessary are actually essential for health.

Silica 47% is bursting with minerals from the earth and can be taken as a rich mineral supplement or used as an effective body cleanser for weight losers. Its silicates help to chelate unwanted elements from the body. Take three to six tablets with water prior to eating. For soothing nutrition try Silica 47%—natural bounty from the earth!

A Word of Caution

Most people don't have time to research nutrition and to be able to evaluate what they read on the labels of products, so here are a few tips in picking your foods. Be sure to read the labels before you buy.

* Some companies label their Spirulina 100% when really there is only 2% Spirulina and the rest is alfalfa or green vegetable powder. Spirulina is in short supply at the moment, which has driven up the price and brought into the market some unscrupulous companies. If you get no results with brands of Spirulina that are not Dr. Hills', you can begin to wonder if you have bought a mislabeled brand. The FDA is now investigating several companies, so hopefully that state of affairs may improve in the near future. We guarantee that every bottle of Light Force Spirulina contains 100% pure Spirulina and *no fillers*.

* Many diet plans feature nice-tasting low-calorie foods which are not as nutritious as they could be nor even as nutritious as claimed. If you get thin on a diet because there is little nutritional value in the products and the added vitamins and minerals are not from natural sources nor chelated by Nature, then you have not only lost weight but also health.

* A cheap product often used is sodium caseinate, quite different from casein, which can be produced by isolating the proteins from milk or soybeans. If it says "Casein" at the top of the list on the label, it means that your good protein is present in a larger quantity than the cheaper ones that are by-products, such as sodium caseinate. Sodium caseinate is full of sodium, which creates water retention in some obese people. Like whey, sodium caseinate can be used as an inexpensive filler.

TO CHANGE YOUR LUCK
IS EASY

There are opportunities every day by which people can change their lives, change their bodies, change their friends, and most of all change their relationship to life. If they are fixed in their habits, narrow in the mind, locked into certain beliefs and concepts, they unwittingly destroy the divine providence (another name for luck) which lies all about them from infancy to old age. If you change inside, your luck will change. If you want to be liberated from the old body and create something new, you must get deeper understanding of both your mind and your body.

The Dr. Hills Slimming Plan offers you an amazing advanced technique in how to control overeating and overweight. However, it does not put you down as some zombie who has no control, with a plan delivered from some high authority, but it puts you in charge of your own destiny. The Dr. Hills Slimming Plan is not only a way to change your life, it is a unique discovery in scientific weight control. By cashing in on this discovery of Spirulina as a superfood, you can now add years to your life, change your life and enjoy a trimmer, more youthful body.

Rejuvenation is not a matter of luck, it is a matter of knowing what is junk. Not only are there "junk foods", but also junk ideas and junk religions, which never deliver luck or happiness because people can't throw them away for something new. The high priests of nutrition who preach the religion of calories really don't have the answer or everyone would be remarkably slim, so why not congratulate yourself right now on your luck? You are going to get rid of junk ideas along with your fat. What happens in your mind hereafter is what will happen in your body, and what has to happen first in your psychological make-up is that you have to be open to everything that is new. This does not mean going overboard and accepting everything new, but testing it out carefully and continuously, proving or disproving it yourself. Don't be daunted by the people who would have you stay just as you are. Determine right now to change your whole outlook on life. You can change everything "out there", everything external including weight, by changing what is "in here", your attitudes, thoughts and ways of looking at yourself.

If you can discover the reason for your present circumstances inside yourself and not blame others or any external situation, then you can accept responsibility now for every mouthful you eat and every ounce of fat you put on, and also accept this wonderful opportunity to begin anew the rejuvenation of your soul as well as your body. The two are not separate, although many religions would have you believe so. Your spiritual life and your material life are all one link with your eternal consciousness. To separate them is not only naive but dangerous to your psychic and physical health. Temptations on the physical level are also temptations on the spiritual level. Once you realize this, you can begin to identify with the best in yourself, your integrity and your honesty, instead of your self-indulgence. Unless you identify with your true self-worth instead of your vanity, your strengths instead of your weaknesses, you will always "cheat" on a diet or even go so far as to structure your life so that you *can* cheat. This is throwing all your divine providence away because when you cheat yourself you cheat your body. Those who hide cookies under the bed to avoid the watchful eyes of friends and family, who do they fool most? Your best self is always going to punish you for cheating it, and you get into a never-ending loop which is writing its own failure in its own consciousness so that the harder you try, the more you cheat yourself of your birthright: a vibrant, healthy, marvellous body which you can live in without feeling guilty about it.

The problem of overweight or overeating is not just fate or ill luck. It is the result of certain chemical imbalances. You can change the natural chemicals in foods you eat by understanding how the amino acids in proteins and the starches and sugars of carbohydrates come together in your body and get suspended in fats. Maybe you don't want to bother to make a study of all the Light Force literature which explains the function of certain pigments or how we metabolize these chemicals. You don't need to do this if you follow the Dr. Hills diet program because it follows the natural laws of eating which have to do with *balance*. Everything in the Universe— the Earth in space, the Sun, and everything under the Sun— eventually must come to a state of balance. This applies to you too. Discover the balance in things and you have discovered the reason why some people are self-defeating and some people have so much good fortune, so much luck with love and life. To lose weight permanently with Dr. Hills weight loss program will open up other opportunities to you that you never knew existed. Spiritually, mentally, and physically you will learn how most diets give only temporary success. You will learn how your mind is responsible for changing your luck.

You are in fact very lucky at this moment because if you have read this far and you really have a problem with self-indulgence, you are going to discover the permanent answer which was sitting inside you all along. This discovery is the real value of this program because no one can take it away from you once you find it. The rejuvenated body is within your grasp because you have now been presented with this opportunity. This Plan is not only the opportunity to become slim yourself but to help others become slim and stay slim by using scientifically formulated Light Force products which give you the energy to change, the energy to exercise and the mental energy to "DO IT NOW".

The Secret of Self-Mastery

When a person makes a decision, deep inside, to become master of himself, it is a very important event, not just a passing phase. It is nothing less than to give up one's identity. Some people see themselves as great lovers; some see themselves as mothers or fathers. Some see themselves as athletes; some as nobodies. It doesn't matter what the identity is, it is "me" and most people have no intention of changing it. If "the eater" is you, then to change it will mean that you become a very different person. But to try to lose weight from inside the eater is like a baby bird trying to fly while it is still inside the hard shell of the egg. If it wants to fly, it will have to break out!

One of my students said she could not lose weight on my Slimming Plan because if she were allowed to eat what she wanted on her free day, then she would eat some more on her "shape up" day. She had to give up her favorite foods completely in order to give them up at all, because she found it impossible to practice any inhibition of her desires. "If I watch one TV show," she said, "pretty soon I am watching six more." A person of this type needs to consider not the possibility of inhibition but the possibility of becoming a *totally different person*. Can this be done? I have many students who have done it. One of them wrote to me recently:

I guess of all your students, I was one of the least willing to change. I was afraid that if I did, I would miss out on living my own special little lifetime and I would not find happiness. But I did change, and I feel like a very different person now. Sometimes the new me feels like an old cathedral with several of the walls crumbled away. It feels *open* and it stands in a sunny meadow with a lovely breeze blowing through. It feels good!

Another wrote:

I never would have grown in the area of communication had it not been for your encouragements. I used to be so blocked, I couldn't express anything without getting supremely embarrassed. But each time I forced myself out there, it became easier and easier, and gradually I learned to express myself. I'm so fulfilled to be more open.

I might add that when these two first came to me I thought they were both a lost cause as far as self-discipline was concerned. But I did not try to bully them. I just tried to mirror the fact that their way was not working but mine was. I waited for them to want to change.

Even when people do want to change, they are likely to be wanting it at a superficial level. Deeper down, there is almost a survival instinct that says "stay the same". So at that level we can be very stubborn—even to the point of self-destruction. If one is compulsive about getting what one wants, be it food or some other thing, it feels almost a matter of life or death, so one is not likely to change just on the advice of a book or even a friend. But to continue on a course that is not in tune with one's deepest being will always bring a lesson from Life (the greatest teacher) and its teachings are sometimes very hard. It is better if we can change ourselves before life has to shape us up against our will.

Probably the greatest pitfall for anyone who sincerely wants to change is to do it in the head, instead of taking the time to make a deep change that goes all the way to the roots.

It is tempting to identify with the good, disciplined, wise part of oneself and reject the weak imperfect part. But in order to make a change that will last, you will have to integrate the weak part and change it, not disown it and avoid dealing with it. And this involves some patience, because right in the midst of all your discipline, the weak or greedy or self-deceptive part of you will suddenly appear on the scene, and this will happen again and again. You will be tempted on the one hand to give the whole thing up as a hopeless task and on the other hand to force yourself past the point you can actually sustain. Neither attitude will work. No one can master a deep pattern overnight; only the *decision* can be made in the instant NOW. After that, the manifesting of your resolution is going to take some time. Bit by bit, you will overcome it, if you have truly made that choice, because it is then no longer a matter of trying to push a big rock up a mountain; there is something lifting the rock, from above. This is the kind of work that does not seem like work, because it rewards and fulfills you.

How is Eating Food Similar to Making Love?

Some people identify with their *thoughts* and opinions and are totally out of touch with what they are *feeling*. Others are in touch with feeling but have no awareness of that deeper part of themselves which we call the soul or spirit. Still others are so wrapped up in the spirit that they forget or mistreat the body. But true self-knowledge is the awareness of our body's needs and its signals, our thoughts, feelings, spiritual dimension and every part of us. It is very common for people to deny one part of themselves for the sake of another part. The ascetic mortifies his body for the sake of his soul. The hedonist mortifies his soul for the sake of his body. Some people, who would never think of denying the body's need to excrete wastes, are quite pious about denying its sexual needs. Sexual starvation is one cause of overweight, since the body tries to console itself with food because other physical needs are not being met. This is called "compensation".

Some people experience an extreme tension before mealtime and an intense release once sufficient food is swallowed down. There is a little signal, perhaps a sigh, that shows the mission is accomplished; one is going to survive. Of course it is foolish to think we would not survive if dinner were late or if all we had were just enough, instead of the amount that triggers the signal. But at a feeling level, we are not so rational. Food is a powerful "compensation". When the bell rings we shout "dinner time" and begin to secrete saliva.

The urge to mate is similarly an instinct for survival, built into every created species, just as the urge to eat is also a natural survival instinct, so it is not so very strange that these two instincts may compensate one for the other. A person who is denied, either by life or by wrong thinking, a release of sexual tension, may find this sexual release at the dinner table, even though it will not seem so and he or she may not recognize it as such. One way to deal with a situation like this is to have more compassion for the sexual needs of our bodies. Another way is to release the energy in sports or exercise, if health permits it.

If it is possible that you are one of those people who is substituting one kind of physical gratification for another, the first step is to realize it. Nature did not intend for us to become civilized at the expense of our bodies but rather to become whole and to express love at every level. Many religions teach that sexuality is a material sin, but this is because so many people have forgotten *love* and have sought sexual union only for the pleasure of the senses. Sex is a sin only if one's consciousness is low; the reason we call it "making love" is because love it its real essence, and its purpose is union.

Eating is similar. A greedy person, a sensualist, will eat more than he should and will eat foods his body would never choose. But that does not mean that eating is a sin for someone else whose consciousness is entirely different. The question is not whether or not to eat of the fruits in the garden of paradise. The real question is, "What am I doing with my consciousness? In what spirit do I live, love, eat, work, and play?" Every garden has its serpent who will be the first to tell us we should break the rules.

Of course, if you are too young to be mating or do not have a mate, it would be foolish to try to meet sexual needs at the expense of the rest of your goals and principles. What many people do not realize is that sexual energy can be channeled into work or play or creativity or even worship. Your consciousness can pour itself into any purpose you feel is worthwhile.

Sexual starvation is not the only common cause of overweight. Spiritual starvation is another and emotional starvation is another. If you are so "heady" that you seem to have no feelings at all, the feelings are there, nevertheless, even though you don't feel them. They lead their own life, hidden in the depths of your unconscious mind, appearing only in your dreams at night. You may think that it is not your fault if you are unable to feel, but in fact you choose it. And you alone can make the decision to let your feelings into your conscious awareness. One way to tell if you are one of these people is to examine your dreams. Oddly enough in the symbolic language of dreams, to eat means to feel. If you eat something in a dream, it means that you permit yourself to experience it by feeling. If you starve someone in a dream, that someone is you. If our emotions crave nourishment, then it is not surprising that our cells will crave nourishment too, because the body is affected by every thought and feeling that we entertain.

What Are You Doing With Your Consciousness?

The more weight you gain, the more you begin to see food as the last thing you should have, so of course it becomes what you most *want*. Before long, your whole consciousness is on food. At breakfast you are planning lunch; at lunch you plan supper; at supper you are thinking of tomorrow's breakfast. Is food really that wonderful or have you *made* it wonderful by the power of your consciousness? You can make it un-wonderful by the same means. As you take a bit of your favorite fattening food and begin to chew, think to yourself, "It tastes OK, but nothing special." This is not just a trick you are playing with your mind. It is real. This is how we create our reality every day without even knowing it. We invest each experience with powerful suggestions of pleasure and pain. Today your reality revolves around your stomach, but tomorrow it could revolve around your loved one or a creative project or your work. It all depends where you decide to put your consciousness, and you have the freedom to put it high or low. But if you put it low, then you will *be* that. You will have defined yourself. Dare to be great by putting your mind on something great!

The price of setting your life's purpose too low is the haunting feeling of emptiness. Some people try to fill the emptiness with alcohol. Some fill it with frantic activity. Some fill it with food. But there is only one thing that can actually fill the emptiness and that is to begin to manifest your highest potential—not the potential of your neighbor or your brother or your favorite movie star or the president of the United States, but your own potential.

Your better self is the one whose first impulse is to think of others or give to others before your lesser self comes in and says, "Don't be a fool." Does a baby or a kitten or a puppy put you in a sweeter state of consciousness? This is your real self. If you hide the love that you feel for your friends or your family, you have hidden your real identity, not only from them but perhaps even from yourself, and you will start to believe in that cool unemotional self-image you have chosen to present to others. We all learn early in life that love makes us vulnerable, and that people may laugh at us or hurt us in that vulnerable state of mind. So we pretend that we are tougher than we are, and soon we *become* what we pretend. We lose touch with the parts we dare not express and we stop believing in them. But the coverings—whether made of self-images or made of layers of fat or of flesh—only hide the best of us, waiting to be rediscovered.

Meanwhile, the worst part of us is often the one we allow to direct our lives. Perhaps we are vaguely aware that we are drifting along in old ruts and patterns instead of changing them. Some people's stumbling block is idleness. Since there is nothing else to do, they eat. For others, the pitfall is being sociable. The drinks, the food and the conversation are all mixed up together, and to talk without eating seems impossible. But are these really such difficult patterns to change? Don't try to stop eating; instead, stop being idle. If you are caught up in a task that is really interesting, you forget to eat. If your conversation is deep and real, it will be so absorbing that food will seem a distraction instead of an accompaniment.

Perhaps your craving is really a craving for parental approval. If so, then set aside your need for a moment and look at your parents objectively. Do they even have the capacity to understand you and thus perhaps begin to "approve"? Look at *yourself* objectively. Are you manifesting in a way that *you* approve of? If not, can you really expect to get the approval of others, and even if you did, would it help, when you yourself do not approve? By this kind of self-honesty we learn to look at reality not through the filters of hopes and desires and fears and doubts but to see things as they really are and to see ourselves, perhaps for the first time.

Even in your own body, you and you alone are at the controls. In your consciousness send a message to your cells NOW. Tell them you appreciate the work they are doing to keep your body fit. Tell them about the Dr. Hills Slimming Plan and say that you are going to need all their help, because you are going to make some important changes that will greatly benefit them. Do not suppose for one moment that your cells will not hear you, for your body is one connected whole, and every cell has its own intelligence and knows how to perform its own body function perfectly. Make friends with your cells and work with them. You will notice a difference in the way you feel.

But this does not mean that your conscious mind is omnipotent. Your consciousness includes also the part of your mind that is *un*-conscious. And because of this, your new way of dieting will require humility. When a dieter pumps up his will power to the point where he is ready to start a diet, he says to himself, "I can do it." His estimation of what "I" can do is usually exaggerated. If instead he had the humility to say, "I've never been able to really do it," then he could ask for help. If he is not a religious person, he cannot ask for God's help, but he can certainly ask the help of whatever part of him keeps his body running and digests his food and heals his wounds for him. This mysterious Intelligence works for us day and night, keeping our hearts beating and our lungs breathing. If we ask this deeper part of ourself to help us gain self-mastery and to help us lose weight, it will not refuse. But this part of us is not impetuous. It will take us to our goal step by step (with our cooperation), and we will have to give it time. Our minds leap ahead to the end result, so we get discouraged that it is not happening in the body as fast as it happens in consciousness. But whether the results are visible or not, that goal is pulling us toward it, and changes are happening in our bodies *before* we are able to see them. At the same time, changes are happening in our psychology. We are building something not just for now but something that endures. We will have it with us the rest of our lives. That "something" is character. It cannot be bought or stolen or bestowed. It can only be built. You may not even realize what is happening until one day it hits you and you see in your own eyes a new strength and a new freedom.

Understanding Your Imagination

People regard imagination as the faculty of unreal and illusory perceptions. But really the imagination is the most powerful aspect of your consciousness and it has the power to literally remake your physical body in accordance with the image you hold in your mind's eye. So if you have a negative self-image, you will perpetuate it year after year until you realize you can change it. Once you change it, your body and personality will conform to the new you, and your posture, the way you move, the way you speak and other attributes will automatically change.

The commitment to change, which you make at the start of this Slimming Plan is a commitment to self-mastery. In order to harness the full power of your imagination, you will have to master the images you create. You will have to keep your imagination positive and never indulge in fear, worry or any imagined negativity. Your commitment is to re-create yourself, and you are going to need all the resources of your consciousness for that transformation, so you cannot afford to let your imagination drain away its precious energy in vain or futile activities. If your commitment is real, you are looking at yourself not in terms of the past but in terms of possibilities and untapped potentials. Do not overrate yourself, but look honestly at the positive qualities you really do have. These can be developed through the power of your imagination to create a new reality by expanding your awareness of who you are. Employ this faculty of imagination as often as you can. Commit yourself to the mastery of it. Once tapped, it will be your servant for life.

To prepare the way for the new you, there are three things you must do.

1. Build habits of nutritious eating. This will give your body the tools it needs to sculpt your new figure just as an artist carves a beautiful form from a block of wood.

2. Wipe out the memory of who you have been up to now, including all the things that people have said you were and all that you have said to yourself to keep yourself confined to a pigeon-hole you never belonged in, in the first place.

3. Visualize the kind of person you want to be—physically, mentally, and spiritually. Beware of misusing the power of your consciousness for low motives. If you visualize yourself in a form that is not in tune with your highest nature, your plan will backfire and cause you some pain. In order for your new vision of yourself to penetrate deep into your mind, rather than staying at the surface, where it will have no power to transform, try to practice the visualization when you are re-laxed and open—for example, as you fall asleep

at night or just as you start to awaken in the
morning. It is best to pick an image which you
feel to be in line with your true being. If you
want to be the opposite of what you really are, you
are lost before you even begin. Your true potential
may be to be intellectually brilliant or it may be
to have a loving heart. You will have to tune into
your own potential to discover the outlines of your
future self. And the same is true at the physical
level. It would be a terrible waste of consciousness
to put a lot of energy into changing your hair
from curly to straight or from straight to curly.
But to reduce your size to the normal beautiful
proportions that are your birthright cannot help
but be in tune with your real nature.

REMEMBER

* Overweight is not just ill fate or bad luck; you have the
power to change it by seeking out its causes.

* It is possible to change yourself into a totally different
person. This has been done.

* For many people, eating is a "compensation" for some
other kind of fulfillment. We can ask ourselves if we have
any area of our lives where we feel a lack or feel some
emptiness or deprivation.

* Little by little we can discover who we really are, beneath
the images of who we think we are or feel we should be.
We can become ourselves—unique and beautiful. To do
any less is to be like a carrot wishing it were a cabbage.

* Your imagination is the doorway to discovery of your real
potential as a person.

DO YOU REALLY WANT TO COUNT CALORIES?

A section of this book is devoted to calorie counters for people who have read all the diet books who have been taught to count calories. They need to understand calories once and for all so that they know why they count. The object is to be free of diet books. After doing exactly what the books tell them and still remaining fat, you would think people would stop buying them, but people so want to be thin, they keep on trying. We will devote a section at the end of the Plan to low-calorie foods, but if you follow the three days of "free days" and the four "shape up" days, you won't need it.

The old way of counting calories I call "poverty consciousness". It is like someone counting pennies to see if there is enough money in the house to buy food. And it produces about the same feeling that somehow there is not going to be enough and that it is not going to be filling. There is an anxiety or an insecurity in counting out the amount you will have to be satisfied with, even though your desire is for much much more. The new way of counting calories is "the way of abundance". It is achieved by knowing in your heart with absolute certainty and faith that there is going to be enough, and that *all you need is enough*! How are you so sure there will be an abundance? By realizing that there are plenty of foods which are delicious and filling and which keep you feeling full for a long time yet are not overly fattening. The only thing you need to avoid as a category of foods is fat.

The body runs by natural laws, regardless of man-made units of measurement. The calorie does not exist in any real scientific sense. It is a measure, like a yardstick or a foot. There are no actual yardsticks or feet in nature, and there are no calories. The calorie is a unit of heat measurement. In exact scientific terms, a calorie is the amount of heat needed to raise the temperature of one kilogram of water one degree centigrade at sea level. When used by dieters, the calories refer to the energy produced by food when oxidized by the body. A gram of carbohydrate is not a theoretical measurement unit like a calorie but refers to something actual and finite in nature. This tangible gram of carbohydrate or gram of protein refers to a gram of organic compounds composed of carbon, hydrogen (carbohydrate), oxygen, sugar, starch, cellulose or amino acids. These are the elements our bodies need, whereas a calorie we only use as a convenience to help us in our selection of foods.

The Dr. Hills Slimming Plan does not argue about proteins or carbohydrates or calories. According to the Plan, a food is only fattening if a person is already overweight. Anything can fatten if your metabolism is out of balance. Regardless of the number of calories, your food assimilation is only fattening if you have been eating wrongly. *Low calorie* food added to a full diet is fattening, and high calorie food added to *low intake* may not fatten you at all. No two individuals need exactly the same calories because the food your system burns as fuel depends on each person's digestion and assimilation. It is here that Dr. Hills' slimming theory is borne out in practice. Digestion and assimilation are aided by certain enzymes triggered by biliproteins and pigments produced in the liver and sent to the intestines. Fortunately, these pigments occur naturally in Spirulina.

Calories Explained

The storage of unused energy in fat or in the cells and tissues of people who cannot burn it in their metabolic processes becomes a real problem if we cannot understand the caloric mechanism.

Actually proteins and carbohydrates contain roughly the same amount of calories. But according to most authorities in diet and nutrition, carbohydrates are supposed to contain *more* calories than proteins do. This is not true. Many people forget that the body uses many of the calories of a protein to convert that protein into muscles and cells while carbohydrate is directly converted more rapidly into glucose and glycogen for producing immediate energy. The body needs an enormous amount of energy to supply the millions of cells with the energy to metabolize proteins, and this is where most of the calories in proteins are consumed. However, if we already have a surplus of stored energy in sugars, starches and fats in the body as a whole, then even the calories in proteins wil be fattening to that person. Therefore the ruling that proteins are not fattening and that proteins are low-calorie food and that the calories in carbohydrates are fattening is false, because *both* are fattening when the body does not burn away its excess calories.

The calories in a particular food depend on the functioning of the whole body the food is going into, whether it will raise that body's energy level or not. Obviously, putting more calories into a body whose cells are actively engaged in oxidation through exercise will only go to resupply those used up, thereby returning to a balanced situation. Putting calories into a clogged system only clogs it further. When there is a *lack* of calories, one sees the body's proteins being consumed for energy purposes in the same way that carbohydrates are used, eventually reducing the cells and muscles to a state like we see in the pictures of malnourished children in refugee camps—usually attributed to protein starvation. Obviously the body can only use the amino acids and sugars and starches that it receives. But as a chemical factory, it is quite ingenious in using both proteins *and* carbohydrates not only to *store* energy but to *use* it.

While fad diets make their programs seem special by restricting you to certain foods and excluding many others with high calories the Dr. Hills Slimming Plan is wide-ranging. Most diets base their program on a single food. More than fifty-one diets are presently based on eggs and grapefruit alone! How boring can you get? You will certainly lose weight if you get bored with the diet, but you may also get hungrier, because boredom itself will produce the desire to eat and eat as a compensation.

There have been a number of recent diets which the FDA and various authorities have warned against. They have even called them dangerous, as they may be lacking in sufficient calories and nutrition. The minimum calories recommended for a low-calorie diet is about 1200. If one is on a low-carbohydrate diet (in order to reduce calories), the average amount recommended is about 60 grams of carbohydrate. But if you are watching your carbohydrate intake on a low-carbohydrate diet and also counting calories, then you discover that many proteins such as beef or eggs have plenty of calories even though they have low carbohydrates. And this means that the breadth of selection you might have on a low-carbohydrate diet is severely narrowed if you must try to also avoid calories. For example, a serving of corned beef has 425 calories—about a third of the daily calorie allowance for a diet of 1200 calories. So according to the low-carbohydrate diet you could eat corned beef all day, but if you also wanted to stay below the 1200 calories, all you could eat would be three helpings of corned beef of 425 calories each and you would already be over this standard amount (1200).

The calorie counting diet is so confusing and so far removed from the actual process of metabolism that Dr. Hills Slimming Plan prefers to balance the calorie intake by eating three days without counting calories and four days on the special supplements that supply just the right amounts of nutrition to give you surplus energy. You will feel this energy, so don't let anyone kid you or blind you with so-called "scientific" facts, which tell you you are not getting enough caloric energy. Calorie counting never made anyone thin!

The Dr. Hills Slimming Plan was formulated to avoid the major problem of low-calorie diets which usually prevent you from eating many different kinds of foods. The Dr. Hills Slimming Plan does not have to contend with this disadvantage of the low-calorie diet. When you eat low-calorie foods on a low-carbohydrate diet, the problem comes when you *do* eat any food high in carbohydrates, because then a large weight gain will result, *totally out of proportion to the caloric value of the food you are eating.* This is due to the metabolic interactions in the body's conversion of fats, starches and sugars, leading to salt and water retention which will delay your weight loss and maybe even give you a weight gain, rather than a weight loss.

Most doctors and nutritionists say that any less than a daily intake of 30 grams of carbohydrate or 800 mixed calories a day could be dangerous to your health, although many doctors may recommend a medically supervised diet much less than that, for other reasons when there is a specific problem. For this reason you should always check with your doctor if you have a physical problem or have poor health before going on a diet.

LOW-FAT HALL OF FAME

The following foods are listed for their contribution of zero to very low amounts of fat within your diet. Many of these foods contain high amounts of vitamins and minerals necessary for your body's needs. Remember, the following food supplements are particularly helpful and can be eaten in combination with other foods on the list:

Spirulina—65-70% protein with 16% carbohydrates
Fiber-Lean—40-60% protein with galactomannans
Bee Pollen—with 20 amino acids
Manna Powder—90% soy protein isolated from soybeans
with added methionine

Apples	Cranberry juice	Peppers
Apple butter	Cucumbers	Pineapple
Apple juice	Dates	Plums
Applesauce	Egg whites	Potatoes
Apricots	Eggplant	Prunes
Asparagus	Endive	Pumpkin
Banana	Farina	Radishes
Barley	Figs	Raisins
Beans, except soybeans	Garden peas	Raspberries
Bean sprouts	Grapefruit	Rice, brown
Beets	Kale	Rice cereal
Blackberries	Lettuce	Rutabagas
Blueberries	Lobster	Sauerkraut
Boysenberries	Lychee nuts	Scallops, steamed
Broccoli	Mangoes	Sherbet
Bulgar	Milk, skim or non-fat	Shrimp
Buttermilk made	Mushrooms	Spinach
from skim milk	Honeydew melon	Squash
Cabbage	Mustard greens	Strawberries
Carrots	Nectarines	Sweet potatoes
Cauliflower	Noodles	Tangerines
Cottage cheese (low-fat)	Oat flakes	Tapioca
Cherries	Oatmeal	Tomatoes
Chestnuts	Okra	Tomato juice
Chicken, light meat, no skin	Onions	Tuna, water-packed
Chickpeas	Oranges	Turkey, light meat, no skin
Codfish	Papaya	Turnips
Collard greens	Parsnips	Turnip greens
Corn	Peaches	Mixed vegetables
Crab	Pears	Watermelon
Cranberries	Peas	Wheat cereal
		Zwieback

Why Avoid Fats?

Your body actually needs some fats in order to function, even if you are already fat. But don't worry about not getting enough. Even if you try, you cannot avoid fat altogether. Nearly everything you look at, including vegetables, has some fat. Since you can't escape fat, it becomes important to take off some of the fat you have already accumulated. Some people believe that one must have a certain amount of fat in the diet in order to be nutritionally complete, but this is not true. If there is no fat in the diet, the body burns its own fat and if there is no fat to burn, it will burn its protein. If we are talking about fatty acids being one of the nutrients that the body needs, that is a different matter entirely, but fatty acids are not fats. You will find linoleic and linolenic fatty acids in Spirulina.

While carbohydrates and proteins contain about equal amounts of calories (about four calories per gram), the amount in fats is over double, at 9.4 calories per gram. While the body can adjust itself to handle surplus carbohydrates and proteins and even swap them if there is a surplus in the body, the situation with fats is different. The key to Dr. Hills Slimming Plan is this. On your free days, eat as much as you like if you can avoid fats. You cannot entirely avoid fats, however, because everything from meat to butter, avocado to peanuts, ice cream to french fries are all loaded. Fat metabolism is different because 45% of the American diet is from fats and oils. If you can get wise to fats and oils, once you have "shaped up" on Dr. Hills' slimming diet plan, you can eat normally so that your "free days" increase in number. By avoiding fats as much as you can, you hasten the day of the ultimate "shape up" by 45%.

REMEMBER

* Calorie counting is based on the assumption that you are self-indulgent and must therefore deprive yourself in order to lose weight. It is like trying to live on a 1935 budget in 1982.

* Dr. Hills Slimming Plan is based on the idea that your spirit is ready and willing to change and, with a little help, will do it. There is no need for deprivation.

* Sometimes low-calorie food is fattening and sometimes high-calorie food is nonfattening; it all depends on the person and the circumstances.

* To rely on calorie-counting is the pathway to failure.

* If you eat low-calorie foods on a low-carbohydrate diet and then you eat a food high in carbohydrates, a large weight gain will result, totally out of proportion to the number of calories in that food.

* Many of the rules of dieting that people have been following for years are ignorant of the basic facts of the way your body metabolizes food and creates energy.

* Since your goal is *to burn stored fat,* you should avoid eating foods that contain fat.

CHARTING

People laugh at their fat friends who say, "I have such a small appetite. I only nibble here and there." But who stops to ask why they say this? Perhaps it is because they really intend to eat very little and they try not to eat, but they don't realize how all the little bits add up. For some types of people, charting can help. In the following pages you will find many different kinds of charts which you can use or not use, depending on whether or not they work for you.

The "Mirror of Your Thinking" Chart

Once your thoughts and attitudes are "brought to light" so that you become fully conscious of them, they lose their power to govern your actions without your permission. It is amazing how this works. All of us have little half-conscious thoughts that go by unnoticed, almost as if we were on "automatic", the way we drive a car without being fully conscious of all our reflex movements of eyes and feet and hands. These little thoughts may go something like this:

Nobody loves me . . . . I'll eat
I never get to go anywhere . . . . I'll eat
Why me? . . . . I'll eat
I think I'll "treat" myself. . . . . I'll eat
I'm no good . . . . I'll eat
I deserve something nice . . . . I'll eat
It's not fair. . . . . I'll eat
I'm lonely . . . . I'll eat
I guess I should— . . . . I'll eat
Work, work, work . . . . I'll eat
You gotta do *some*thing! . . . . I'll eat
I'm bored. . . . . I'll eat
I can't help it. . . . . I'll eat
My mother . . . . I'll eat
I feel so bad I want to cheer myself up . . . I'll eat
I wish I were handsome. . . . . I'll eat
I'm tired. . . . . I'll eat
I don't want to be too skinny. I kind of like
   a voluptuous figure . . . . I'll eat

The "Mirror of Your Thinking" chart has four divisions:
   1. THOUGHTS, FEELINGS, AND ATTITUDES
   2. DECISIONS ON HOW TO CHANGE YOUR LIFE
   3. EFFECTS OF THESE DECISIONS
   4. REVISIONS OF THE DECISIONS

Some examples of the kind of decisions you might make
are:
   I'm going to get a new job.
   OK, no more cookies for a month.
   I'm going to call my friends and cheer myself up.
   From now on I'm going to care for myself—and
      in a different way from eating!
   I'm going to clean my house and fix it up.
   I'm going to start exercising before breakfast
      five days a week.

What I need is to get out more.
I'm going to take a class.
From now on, one Spirulina supper per week—
    minimum!

Whatever steps you take to implement these decisions will produce effects in your life, for better or for worse, and these you list in the "Effects" column. If you've tried something too ambitious, you may experience a backlash and find yourself in worse shape than before. Only then would you fill out the "Revision" column and try again. The reason for listing both positive and negative effects in the "Effects" column will soon become apparent; you begin to see how even the smallest decisions that you make can affect your life very powerfully, and you can see your track record on your chart. So be sure to put not only effects on yourself but also effects on the lives of others around you, because these are your best mirror of who you are and what kind of life you are creating.

The "Mirror of Your Thinking" chart will take you to the reality of whatever situation you are in. It will show you not only the way you relate to others but also your inner world, which may be a different portrait entirely. If for example, you look closely at a feeling of discouragement inside you, you may see that it comes from years of trying one diet after another whose results proved to be only temporary. And the feeling comes, "Am I going to diet my whole life away?" Here is one way your chart can help you. If the "Thoughts" column is mainly filled with thoughts about yourself and only a slight mention of anyone else, it may be that cookies loom larger in your life than people do. What heightens their value out of proportion?

The following is a letter from a student of mine who learned a very powerful lesson during a prolonged illness:

> When I was sick I pulled away from friends and concentrated on my own problem of getting myself well. I often thought to myself, "Isn't it amazing that in all this time alone, I haven't been lonely at all?" I was proud to be so self-sufficient. But little by little I began to get in touch with how much I was depending on my boyfriend. He was too busy to come and visit very often and I was getting more and more upset until I finally realized how desperately I needed him. All the long days and long evenings alone, while I was thinking I was only bored but not lonely, I was really very, very LONELY!! Why didn't I know it? Because I filled the time with television and was busy thinking what to eat, when to take my pills, how to get my laundry done, etc.
>
> Now I begin to wonder if I have done the same for years—focusing on what is fun to eat and on my favorite shows on TV—seeking nourishment in things that do not really nourish. While I was sick I got a chance to take my life's values to their total extreme, and after awhile they all seemed hollow. Even my favorite TV show began to seem shallow. However good it was, it could not give me what I needed. It was like trying to eat a tin can.

This case is extreme but it illustrates a point: that our habitual values may be 180 degrees away from reality. Sickness and crisis bring us to the common denominator of our humanity where we have bodily needs that candy and cookies cannot meet, emotional needs that television cannot fill, and spiritual needs that can only be met by getting ourselves in tune with the timeless laws of our own nature and our own consciousness.

THE MIRROR OF YOUR THINKING

Date	Thoughts, Feelings, and Attitudes	Decisions	Effects	Revisions

Biofeedback Chart

You can exercise like someone flinging out a handful of seeds but not bothering to watch them come up, or you can reap the fulfillment of watching your efforts bear fruit. Your body will give you feedback on your attempts to nourish it and give it exercise. If you overdo, the feedback will be negative. If you treat your body with respect, it will express to you its gratitude. And you will notice psychological effects as well. The "Biofeedback Chart" can help you see clear patterns in whether the kinds of exercise you do are right for you and also the spirit in which you do them. By charting your progress you can give your body more of what it needs and less of what it doesn't need. What you need may be different from what you want. But once we find health, energy, and spiritual well-being, often the other things we seek are magically drawn to us, like a magnet.

BIOFEEDBACK

Day	Kind of Exercise	Time Spent	Attitude Before, During, and After Exercising	Physical and/or Psychological Effects	Other Comments
Mon.					
Tues.					
Wed.					
Thurs.					
Fri.					
Sat.					
Sun.					

END OF THE WEEK: LONG TERM EFFECTS

Date	

A Picture is Worth a Thousand Words

The following is a standard chart of desirable weights for people, based on their height and the size of their body frame:

DESIRABLE WEIGHTS FOR MEN
OF AGES 25 AND OVER*
Weight in Pounds According to Frame (In Indoor Clothing)

Height (with shoes on) 1-inch heels		Small Frame	Medium Frame	Large Frame
Feet	Inches			
5	2	112-120	118-129	126-141
5	3	115-123	121-133	129-144
5	4	118-126	124-136	132-148
5	5	121-129	127-139	135-152
5	6	124-133	130-143	138-156
5	7	128-137	134-147	142-161
5	8	132-141	138-152	147-166
5	9	136-145	142-156	151-170
5	10	140-150	146-160	155-174
5	11	144-154	150-165	159-179
6	0	148-158	154-170	164-184
6	1	152-162	158-175	168-189
6	2	156-167	162-180	173-194
6	3	160-171	167-185	178-199
6	4	164-175	172-190	182-204

*Metropolitan Life Insurance Company, New York.

DESIRABLE WEIGHTS FOR WOMEN
OF AGES 25 AND OVER*†
Weight in Pounds According to Frame (In Indoor Clothing)

Height (with shoes on) 2-inch heels		Small Frame	Medium Frame	Large
Feet	Inches			
4	10	92-98	96-107	104-119
4	11	94-101	98-110	106-122
5	0	96-104	101-113	109-125
5	1	99-107	104-116	112-128
5	2	102-110	107-119	115-131
5	3	105-113	110-122	118-134
5	4	108-116	113-126	121-138
5	5	111-119	116-130	125-142
5	6	114-123	120-135	129-146
5	7	118-127	124-139	133-150
5	8	122-131	128-143	137-154
5	9	126-135	132-147	141-158
5	10	130-140	136-151	145-163
5	11	134-144	140-155	149-168
6	0	138-148	144-159	153-173

Metropolitan Life Insurance Company, New York.
†*For girls between 18 and 25, subtract 1 pound for each year under 25.*

But the same amount of weight can be distributed on the body frame in many different ways, some more attractive than others. So body measurement may be more important to our ideals of beauty than is body weight. If we set out our goals in a general way (e.g., "I want to reduce the size of my upper arms, thighs, and stomach" or "I want to get rid of my double chin and my big hips and to have a waist that goes in instead of out") we can map our progress by measuring our arms, legs, waist, hips, etc. We can measure it with a tape measure or measure it with our eyes by looking in the mirror.

The day you begin your diet, xerox ten or twenty copies of the following page and on one of them write the date and your goals. Sketch a picture of how you feel you look on this day. Also make an "ideal shape" page for the figure you want to create and date that page some time in the future. Each week while you are dieting, take a new sheet and redraw yourself in the new form that you see in the mirror. If your weight loss is not reducing the part of you that you want to make smaller, devise an exercise for that part. Notate on the picture-page that you are starting to work on that part. Next week's picture will show the effects.

By the time you finish your diet, the pictures will tell you what a tremendous thing you have accomplished, and you can feel justifiably proud of it, for there is the evidence right before your eyes, in case you have forgotten where you started and how far you have actually come.

DATE: _____

Comments: _____

_____

_____

_____

_____

_____

Keeping Track of Where It Went

One way of giving yourself the recognition you deserve for your efforts is to keep track of your progress on a graph. You would put your starting weight in the upper left corner of the graph and in the rectangle beneath it you would put that same weight minus one pound. Continue on down the left column always subtracting one pound for each rectangle. Your left column might look something like this:

165
164
163
162
161
160
159
etc.

Having put your starting weight in the left column, you would not fill in your first weight-loss number until the following week, and you would put it in the column for "week one". After several weeks, your graph might look something like this:

	Week 1	Week 2	Week 3	Week 4	Week 5	Week 6	Week 7	Week 8
165								
164								
163								
162								
161								
160								
159								
158								
157								
156								
155								
154								
153								
152								
151								
150								
149								
148								
147								

KEEPING TRACK OF WHERE IT WENT

	Week 1	Week 2	Week 3	Week 4	Week 5	Week 6	Week 7	Week 8	Week 9	Week 10	Week 11	Week 12	

The Process of Self-Discovery

In the same way that you can graph your loss of pounds, you can also get a picture of how much you are changing in other ways. In fact, if you do not keep track of it, you may never realize how much you are changing as you follow the Dr. Hills program for self-mastery. On the basis of how you feel about yourself and the comments made by others, you can estimate your progress on a scale of zero to ten. By xeroxing the chart, you can use it for several different qualities at once, for example:

1. Self-acceptance
   Self-respect
   Self-worth
   Self-love

2. Openness
   Being Real
   Being in Touch
      with Feelings

3. Communi-
      cation
   Connectedness
   with others

4. Fulfillment
   Selflessness
   Giving

5. Integrity
   Responsibility

In order to estimate how much you have changed in any of these categories (or other categories you might use for yourself), you will have to watch the kinds of thoughts which go through your mind almost too quickly to be noticed. Jot down in the space provided on the chart the incidents or thoughts which governed your estimate, and this will show you why you slipped back or how you broke through to new spaces, while the graph shows you how much.

This graph can be used on a daily, weekly or monthly basis, but whichever you choose, stick to it. If it is weekly, then make a notation once a week. There is not a great deal of room for writing, so you will need to express your experience in capsule form. This will give a clarity that more words would only obscure, and you will be able to tell by a glance at your chart where you have been and what you have achieved.

You will write in only one rectangle of space, because that is the way you make your progress visible on the scale of zero (worst) to ten (best). Your chart might look something like this:

QUALITY: SELF-WORTH

	7–4–82	7–11–82	7–18–82
10			
9			
8			
7			
6			
5			
4			Am getting slim!
3			
2		Didn't let J. get me down	
1			
0	"I can't look anyone in the eye"		

THE PROCESS OF SELF-DISCOVERY

Quality: _____

DATE ➡				
10				
9				
8				
7				
6				
5				
4				
3				
2				
1				
0				

PART II

FOR THOSE WHO WANT MORE

(Part II of the Dr. Hills Slimming Plan offers facts and technical information for those who are interested in going deeper. If, however, you are satiated with words and ready to start practicing the alternating free and shape up days, then you can skip Part II and still do very well with the slimming).

CHAPTER 14

RECIPES FOR YOUR SHAPE UP DAY

COLD DRINKS WITH SPIRULINA*

Delicious Smoothie

Put ½ to 1 cup apple juice in blender (depending on how thick you want the smoothie to be).

Start blender and into the vortex, drop 2 rounded teaspoons of Spirulina Powder. (To begin this way keeps the powder from sticking to the sides of the blender.)

Chop in 1 apple and 1 banana.

Optional: other fruits such as blackberries add a lot of flavor.

This makes a thick rich wonderful meal-in-itself. Serves one or more.

Fiber-Lean Smoothie

3 cups apple juice
2 frozen bananas
1½ tbsp. Spirulina Powder
Up to 1 level tbsp. Fiber-Lean

Serves 3.

Green Tara

1 peach
1 apple
1 pear
1 glass pineapple juice
1 tbsp. Spirulina

Blend all ingredients in blender. Serves one or more.

You can make smoothies or just mix your Spirulina Powder with juice, using apple juice, carrot juice, fresh squeezed orange juice, V-8 or tomato juice with a dash of Tabasco. Spirulina is also good with pineapple juice.

Sparkling Apple Cider

⅔ cup apple juice
⅓ cup sparkling water
1tsp. or more of Spirulina Powder

Blend in blender. Makes a cool, bubbly summertime drink.

Gazpacho Blend

1 large ripe tomato (sliced)
½ cucumber (unpeeled)
1 or 2 green onions
1 cup vegetable juice
1 tbsp. Fiber-Lean
1 heaping tsp. 100% Spirulina Powder

Blend, chill and eat with spoon and crunchy Nibblesticks.

Strawberry Smoothie Delight

1 cup frozen strawberries
½ frozen banana
½ cup frozen peaches or any other fruit
1 cup apple juice
¼ cup water
1 heaping tsp. Spirulina
1 level tbsp. Fiber-Lean

Blend and enjoy!

*A smoothie can range in calories from 243 to 156 with 1 cup juice and ½ fruit or ½ cup fruit depending on the juice and the fruit chosen. If you like grape juice, for example, use a smaller amount.

Frozen Wonder

½ cup canned diet pears or fresh pears if in season
1 cup frozen strawberries
1 cup apple juice
1 level tbsp. Fiber-Lean
1 heaping tsp. Spirulina

Blend in blender.

Tropical Smoothie

1 cup papaya juice or mango juice
½ frozen banana
½ cup pineapple
1 level tbsp. Fiber-Lean
1 heaping tsp. Spirulina

Blend in blender.

Sumptuous Shake

1 cup nonfat milk
1 frozen banana
dash of vanilla extract
1 level tbsp. Fiber-Lean

Whip into frothy delight and garnish with nutmeg.

Morning Goodness

1½ cups melon
1 frozen banana
¼ cup water
1 level tbsp. Fiber-Lean

Blend in blender.

HOT DRINKS WITH SPIRULINA

Spirulina with Apple Juice

Try heating the apple juice, adding a dash of cinnamon and a teaspoon of nutritional (not bakers') yeast. The amount of Spirulina will vary to taste. Add the Spirulina after you take the apple juice off the heat.

Busy Day Soup

1 qt. V-8 juice
½ cup instant onion
1 tbsp. Spirulina Powder

Combine all ingredients and heat but do no boil.

Combine all ingredients and heat but do not boil.

Serves 4.

Variation: omit the onion or reduce to 1 tablespoon and season the soup with a touch of Dr. Hills West Indian Seasoning.

Spirulina Miso Soup

Pour into a blender 1½ cups water
Add a generous spoonful of miso
Blend.
Add a generous spoonful of Spirulina Powder—at least 1 tablespoonful. Blend again.
Heat gently but *do not boil*. If desired, you can add cayenne and/or nutritional yeast.

Serves one.

Hot or Cold Soup

8–12 oz. tomato juice cocktail or V-8 or consommé
1 tsp. Lecithin^{Plus}
1 level tsp. Fiber-Lean
1 heaping tsp. 100% Spirulina Powder
garlic (optional)
cayenne pepper or hot sauce (optional)

Blend in a blender til smooth. If you heat it, remember not to boil Spirulina.

On the run: you can make up a large batch to meet your three-times a day requirements by tripling the amount of the ingredients and drinking ⅓ at each mealtime.

Zesty Zucchini Soup

2 to 3 large zucchini, sliced
2 cups water
one tbsp. vegetable broth
Dr. Hills West Indian Seasoning, a dash
¼ cup dry nonfat milk
1 tbsp. Fiber-Lean
1 tbsp. Spirulina
(optional: 1 tbsp. Lecithin^{Plus})

Simmer first four ingredients. Add the rest, pour into blender (a warmed blender) and whip. Sprinkle parmesan cheese over the top, garnish with chopped green onions or parsley flakes. Makes 2–3 servings depending on size of zucchini.

SPIRULINA AND ENERGY

Joggers and athletes are practical people who try to increase their energy levels through diet. They experiment and, like the health food trade, go through crazes. Before the present interest in carbohydrates for the delivery of muscular energy, the rage was to eat as much protein as possible. Now protein is out of favor, which reveals that many of these people go from one thing to another without fully understanding the metabolic aspects of energy production. But they are not to blame because even people who should know the elementary knowledge of metabolism only have theories to go on.

At universities all over the country, nutritionists and doctors are taught certain standard concepts about amino acids and proteins, as well as the conversion of carbohydrate, starches and sugars into glucose and blood sugars for delivery to muscles and cells. Recently there has been advanced research into the nature of carbohydrates and metabolism which has not yet filtered down to standard university courses, and many of the old time professors of biology are still parroting concepts they learned concerning food values from thirty years ago. Whenever anything new comes out, a host of smatterers descend on it and dissect it with their old ideas—often without any experimental or factual basis. Hence, diet books and theories about weight loss and metabolism of energy and the storage of surplus energy and fat abound and proliferate, because very few people have clear knowledge and experience of what *works*.

With the recent research on the way polysaccharides bond to certain proteins and act as markers for delivery of certain nutrients to the cell, comes the knowledge that all carbohydrates cannot be lumped together and treated as if they produce the same effect on energy levels and cell metabolism. By the same token, work is proceeding on proteins which shows that they are far more complex than was formerly believed, and to lump them together without discriminating their actual functions as energy producers or building blocks becomes a senseless endeavor. It is becoming clear that some proteins can even act as carbohydrates were thought to do; and carbohydrates can act as triggers for protein synthesis.

In my own work with Spirulina, with literally hundreds of thousands of people eating it and receiving a high rate of energy metabolism, we have come to observe that the quality of the proteins or the quality of the carbohydrates is all-important. Even though Spirulina has the highest profile of amino acids and the largest content of protein of any known vegetable, it is the type and quality of those proteins that make it behave in the body almost like a carbohydrate, because the proteins are largely biliproteins, of the type manufactured by the liver in the production of enzymes.

People continually ask what metabolism really is. Basically it is the oxidation of cells or the breathing of our cell life which enables the cell to process the nutrients delivered to it in the blood. The burning of energy by our cells depends on certain oxidants. One of these is the pigment in blood, and others are the biliproteins manufactured by the liver, which trigger enzyme production. The unique thing about Spirulina is that these biliproteins, which normally have to be made by the liver, are already present in the Spirulina.

Proteins contain about the same potential energy as carbohydrates do, gram for gram, but the proteins of most foods have to be broken down into amino acids and then re-formed into new proteins in the body. This means that most of the calories of those foods go into the digestive process itself instead of being made available in ready energy. Spirulina gives you energy quickly, efficiently and directly. You receive an immediate charge of energy which does not suddenly drop off like a sugar reaction but lasts from meal to meal. Normally the body would have to go through its usual metabolic process in which the liver manufactures porphyrin pigments, but since Spirulina contains the pigments, ready-made and ready to go to work, it short-cuts this process in a way that few foods can, since it is very rare to find such a concentration of these pigments in a food.

We are beginning to realize the role of pigments in the body. Pigments color the blood with heme, in the same way that the pigment chlorophyll colors the plant cell—the structure of the molecules (heme and chlorophyll) being almost identical. One carries oxygen to the cell; the other carries carbon dioxide. One is an oxygen source and the other is a carbon source. And both are involved in the oxidation of cells in metabolic processes. Imagine the enriching effect on the blood when chlorophyll-rich Spirulina (which except for one atom in its molecule, is the same as heme in the blood) is taken into the body!

There are also several other pigments in bile and blood, with porphyrin-type structures similar to pigments in marine plants and seaweeds which synthesize light at different depths of the ocean—the blue and green pigments being near the surface and the red pigments, like phycoerythrin, being more sensitive to the longer rays of light at greater depths.

The ability of plant metabolic processes to synthesize these protein pigments in order to use energy and achieve growth and oxidation of the cells and to make starch, can teach us about human metabolism which uses these same pigments stored in vegetable life. In some countries, by eating meat we obtain indirectly those proteins which animals have obtained from plants by eating these protein pigments and carbohydrates. In eating the meat, we do not get the carbohydrate which has been used to provide energy for the animal, but we know from human experience that these concentrated proteins do provide energy, and physical laborers have traditionally "beefed themselves up". In giving Spirulina, however, to physical laborers, we have found its vegetable proteins to give more energy and to last longer than meat proteins do, so that workers have exclaimed about the difference and about how much more work they can do and how much more energy they have on a Spirulina diet. So this forces us to look for the cause, since it is a common experience, not only among laborers but among people who get tired and drowsy after meals and in the afternoon, that a few grams of Spirulina per day on a regular basis will, after a few days, make them perky and energetic. And the effect is not only physical but mental, meaning that the brain also gets something that was apparently lacking in the diet.

The problem of getting certain amino acids and complex sugars through the blood-brain barrier, has often been stated in terms of the size of the molecule. However, recent research has shown that it depends upon *which* molecules of sugars are associated together with rare sugars which are made in the body's muco-polysaccharides and enzymes which coat the membranes of the cells causing them to recognize or reject those nutrients which are lacking in some essential feature. Therefore my approach has been to provide all the features possible, through supernutrition, so that the body itself can make any complex enzyme or protein or sugar, because it is now known that if one amino acid or ingredient is missing in the environment of the cell, then that process cannot take place, causing incomplete metabolism. Attributing specific roles to proteins or carbohydrates or fats without regard for their combination as lipo-proteins or proteins associated with certain sugars or carbohydrates has been the mistake of standard nutritionists to date and has led to a situation where most nutritional diets show more speculative theory than actual factual results in increased production of energy, combined with loss of fat.

There has been remarkable neglect by nutritionists concerning the *quality* of different proteins and carbohydrates stored by plants and by animals. The ability to store starches in animal cells, through conversion of glucose to glycogen, to be reconverted into energy when demanded by carbon dioxide levels in the blood, is copied in vegetable plants like Spirulina which are highly energetic organisms, metabolizing at ten times the rate of human beings, and whose lifetimes can be calculated in hours rather than in years and whole metabolic processes can be calculated in seconds rather than in minutes. Is it not strange that a vegetable like Spirulina would store animal starch like glycogen, when it does not have a liver to make it happen? Obviously the plant must side-step the enzyme process in the liver of animals and directly manufacture glycogen. As most plants do not have glycogen or animal starch, except those undergoing rapid energy changes in metabolism, such as blue-green algae, it is no wonder that in eating a vegetable like Spirulina, there is no comparison in energy level to eating a vegetable like lettuce or cabbage. Therefore in achieving higher human energy, one must study the *quality* or *type* of plant or animal protein and not stick labels on everything in simplistic terms which ignore totally the fact that one carbohydrate may be as different to another as it is to a protein.

One must also look more at the synergistic effects of nutrition that can be most easily seen in the effects of glycosides. The well-known effect of specific glycosides, such as belladonna and digitalis, on specific muscles of the human body are examples of types of sugars associated with compounds which produce remarkable energy effects. Similarly, the glycosides in ginseng and Spirulina have specific effects on energy levels of the muscles and metabolism of energy in the body as a whole. Furthermore, it is easy to test these synergistic effects merely by eating one teaspoon of ginseng or Spirulina and walking two to three miles alongside someone who hasn't. This may be too simplistic for some scientific brains, but any experimenter with common sense will discover that if you give an athlete six Spirulina tablets after he's run a marathon, his energy will pick up much faster and if you give him six tablets *before* the marathon, his *speed* of running will be faster. All of this has been tested objectively, even though the smatterers will say it is all *sub*jective in the mind of the runner. Instead of taking six tablets themselves and getting more common sense, they sit in an armchair surrounded by thick books and require so much energy to carry around all the information in their heads that they have no further energy left to make a simple experiment. It is remarkable how much energy the human brain consumes. And I personally am convinced that more people would lose weight if they used their brains and exercised frequently by taking out the tons of clutter in there, which requires a lot more effort than running 26 miles in a marathon.

Taking the right kind of carbodydrate or protein can determine whether we feel emotionally energetic and active or mentally sluggish. It is a fact that active people, who are mentally energetic, work off enough calories to keep their bodies in balance. Therefore the secret of optimum energy metabolism is to eat those things which improve our sense of well-being and to research the rare sugars and carbohydrates rather than the common ones. The rare sugar in Spirulina is rhamnose, which is rare because it is biologically active and is present in many glycosides. Unfortunately there is almost nowhere you can buy it except in the form of Spirulina which has almost ten percent. You could get it by eating poison ivy, but the biologically active compound that comes along with it has notorious effects. You can also get it from bioflavonoids such as rutin and rutinose. These bioflavonoids have well-known effects on blood flow and capillary action. And I have noted many cases of people who complain of cold extremities who feel a change within hours after eating Spirulina. The connection between metabolic processes and the delivery of nutrients at the sites where they are required is the secret of higher energy states.

TOO MUCH SALT?

Keeping sodium in proper balance is the work of the kidneys which in most people excrete any surplus salt. Many people can ingest twelve times their regular sodium intake and excrete it without any problem, but there are many others who cannot, and the salt therefore piles up in the body trapped in the tissue and membranes of our cells.

Americans definitely eat too much salt. This does not mean that salt is bad for proper diets because actually a correct amount is essential to good metabolism. Sodium and potassium are the electrolytes which make the energy transactions in the cell work to exchange ions. Without ion exchange across the membranes of cells, no real health or proper metabolism is possible. The problem is one of *too much* salt and where do you pick it up in your diet without knowing? Most manufactured foods contain a lot of salt because it is the cheapest of all ingredients.

Just putting the salt shaker away in the garbage can does not mean your diet will be free of salt. Nearly all manufactured foods like soups, sauces, canned meats, ham or corned beef are loaded with salt beyond your wildest dreams. But it is no use getting hysterical and joining the latest food fad. The Dr. Hills Slimming Plan looks at salt as dangerous only if your body cannot eliminate it or is overloaded with it already. How do you tell?

Too much salt intake can be seen in your eyes as well as in your swollen tissues. Hypertension and high blood pressure are two things which reflect too much salt. Hypertension is a factor in half the deaths in modern life, and one out of four Americans suffers from high blood pressure, even though they may not know it. It is often symptomless and undetected for years until there is a sudden heart attack or stroke. The intake of salt, or rather the sodium which is in salt, is often the silent accomplice in the deaths of those people unaware of the importance of nutrition in maintaining good health.

The average American today consumes two to two-and-a-half teaspoons of salt per day, and that is twenty times what the body actually needs. About 35 million people suffer from hypertension and, if we include mild cases as well, about 60 million or one-fourth of the population suffer from hypertension. Nearly half of all retired people over 65 years old are also affected by hypertension caused by overuse of salt. The correct intake of sodium per day is now recommended at 200 mg. That is about a pinch as big as your fingernail.

Flushing the Kidneys

Saccharine nitrates, sugar, chemical additives, food colors and artificial flavorings are not the only dangers which have now come under suspicion by doctors. Because of overloading in the diet, doctors and the FDA have been advocating less salt in our diets for years. Doctors have insisted on removal of cyclamates. However, as yet the labeling of sodium content on such items as food packages, soups or antacids is not always implemented by manufacturers. The bureaucrats who protect us from incorrect labeling are strict on many things but not on sodium or salt. The labeling of sodium bicarbonate in cakes, muffins and cooking powders and mixes is still not a priority with the public health agencies. They are more concerned with what you are allowed to read than what you should be allowed to eat. Recently they stopped me from selling an excellent book by medical experts in Japan who had researched Spirulina which has very low sodium content. The problem was that the doctors made medical claims. No medical claims are made for salt, but thousands are literally hooked on it.

Sodium in large amounts will not only clog up your system but will also clog your brain and prevent your memory from working, but still the authorities do nothing about it. Only you, the consumer, can police your own diet and protect your own body by knowing how much salt there is in certain foods. You also need to know how to get rid of salt from the body if you have accumulated it. Remember that salt increases your appetite and makes the body retain water in the tissues. The first objective is to study the list of foods with high salt content; the second is to work hard to eliminate salt.

How to Get Rid of Sodium

The Light Force plan for eliminating salt recommends a hot bath every night, a good soaking to leach sodium and sodium chloride from the body. But you have to realize that at the same time, other minerals and trace elements are also removed through the skin when you do this. These must then be replaced through nutrition. The Light Force family of products are balanced to achieve a higher proportion of potassium to sodium because most modern processed foods contain excessive amounts of sodium chloride. Even sodium ascorbate, often touted by health food enthusiasts as a source of Vitamin C, is also a source of sodium in your diet. Even sodium caseinate, a cheaper form of casein placed into the formulas of many manufactured high protein powders, is a source of sodium to be avoided at all costs in the Dr. Hills Slimming Plan.

The following list covers foods which contain high amounts of salt (sodium). These are foods which you should not necessarily avoid but you should definitely be watching, because in weight reduction you can prevent water retention by being wary of too much salt.

SALT LIST

All commercial soups
Broth
Canned bouillon or cubes
Consommé
Gravy
Catsup
Prepared mustard
Any meat sauce
Soy sauce
Worcestershire sauce
Steak sauce
Chili sauce
Kitchen Bouquet
Horseradish
Cured meats (ham, bacon, corned beef)
Cheese
Bread

Chipped beef
Wieners
Luncheon meats
Bologna
Canned salmon
Monosodium glutamate
Seasoned salts (celery, garlic)
Pickles
Olives
Sauerkraut
Salted crackers
Pretzels
Potato chips
Salted nuts
Salted popcorn
Buttermilk
Peanut butter
Chewing tobacco

COMBINED SALT AND/OR SUGAR LIST

There are certain rules for making the Slimming Plan work, which are simple for weight losers to observe. One is to avoid the items on the following lists which contain combinations of salt (or sugar) in excess. Another is to learn to read labels carefully.

Foods

Anchovies
Pretzels
Pickles
Olives in brine
Chocolate pudding
Cheese
Bread
Waffles
Canned peas and corn
Most canned vegetables
English muffins
Fast foods, TV and chicken dinners, jumbo burgers, etc.

Dry milk, bacon and ham
Tuna pie
Soy sauce
Salted butter and margarine
Commercial salad dressings
Frozen pies
Instant potatoes
Beef jerky
Salt fish

Chemicals

Sodium ascorbate
  (Vitamin C substitute)
Sodium caseinate
Sodium bicarbonate
Antacids, e.g., Alka Seltzer

NOTE: Many products of bakeries, soup manufacturers, etc. contain both salt and sugar. Some manufacturers offer salt-free soups, etc. Read labels to avoid sugar and/or salt.

SUGAR:
ILLUSION OR REALITY?

Running your body on sugar is like running your car on its battery instead of on gasoline. More and more, people are eating refined sugar products instead of complex carbohydrates which are rich in micronutrients. They feel a rush of energy from the sugar, so "it must be all right". What feels good to them must also feel good to the body, they think. But what is really happening? The body is getting the energy but not the nutrients it needs to do its work. An extra burden is placed on other nutrients in order to compensate for the emptiness of the refined sugar energy. This results not only in nutritional imbalance but in marginal or severe dietary deficiencies, one feels let down and moody and then craves still more sugar for still more energy. But it is all false. If someone handed you a picture of a steak dinner and said, "Eat this for supper," you would say, "No, it won't fill me, it won't nourish; I want a *real* steak, not a phony one." Yet we are content to eat refined sugar as if it were real food when really it is only a man-made product.

The sugars that occur in foods are either natural constituents of the food, or are generated during processing, or they are intentionally added. In either case, many different sugars may be present. Sucrose has been the totally dominating carbohydrate sweetener for a very long time. With a world production of *over 70 million tons*, this product constitutes a considerable part of the daily calorie intake per person, especially in the developed countries.

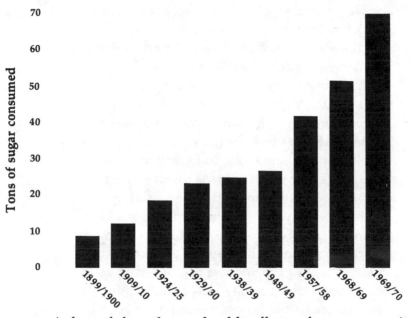

A few of the adverse health effects of sucrose are its contribution to obesity, to dental cavities, the fact that in aberrant metabolism it causes and aggravates diabetes; it is also implicated in hypertriglyceridaemia. But for most people, the effects of sucrose may be invisible. The body is such a wonderful instrument that it hides from us the difficulty it is having in substituting one nutrient for another that is lacking or in just keeping our bodies ready to do whatever we want to do with them. People get so used to a thing like chronic tiredness that it seems normal, but it may really be a serious communication from the body. Tiredness is an illness. Later on, when a worse illness comes, it is too late to give the body the power to ward it off. The following was written by a junk-food addict, a lady forty-four years old:

I never had a serious illness in my life. I never

would take any advice on improving my diet, because I just used my dad's motto, "You can't argue with success!" When I got pneumonia I took it very lightly. It was almost exciting to have such a glamorous disease, and I figured that the antibiotics would knock it out right away and I had nothing to worry about. But the first anti- biotic didn't work. That was OK; I started the second one. I was getting weaker and more exhausted, but I was confident in the medicine. But the second antibiotic did not work either, and the doctor said that I was much worse instead of better. I went home rather confused. If I was worse and they had nothing to make me better, then my own body was going to have to do the work of healing me, but my body was not working right. It was sick. Being too tired to even go to the grocery was a totally new and shocking experience to me. Someone said it was all the junk foods that had brought me to this state, and I got mad. How silly! Of course it wasn't the junk foods. I was doing fine 'til I got this stupid disease. But I did rather wish I had been in better shape before I got it, because maybe I could have put up a better fight. Now I was worse and no options left. As the weeks went by, it occurred to me that I might even actually die during my long battle for health. It was a long time before I managed to get well, and it was a bitter enough experience that it has affected my attitude toward sweets. They are delicious but not worth it. I've made up my mind not to ever get sick again if I can help it.

It is as hard to convince an overeater as it is to convince a junk-food addict that the payoff for bad eating habits is going to be a body that no one wants, including its owner.

"Junk Foods" Taste Yummy

There is a direct link between the physical and psychological events in life. School children cannot learn well today because their foods are full of salt and preservatives which have a disastrous effect on our memory. Adults can't get up the will to change either because the foods are laced with chemicals which sap your energy while the advertising makes you think they are full of nutrition.

Take for instance the breakfast cereal scam. It is based on the fact that sugar costs about 12 cents a pound, actually cheaper than the other ingredients. The pre-sweetening racket creates glucose reactions and insulin problems because 50% of the product is sugar, and the actual cereal has lost most of its vitamins. It's the same with bread. Two slices of bread have more salt than a dill pickle preserved in salt water. Here are the losses of vitamins caused by processing of flour in order to make it taste nice:

Thiamin 80% lost	Niacin 75% lost
Riboflavin 60% lost	Pantothenic acid 50% lost

At the same time those processed foods rob you of essential minerals which your body needs to metabolize fats and proteins . . .

Loss of minerals through refining	Manganese	98% lost
	Iron	80% lost
	Magnesium	75% lost
	Phosphorus	70% lost
	Copper	65% lost
	Calcium	50% lost
	Potassium	50% lost

If we do not get our vitamins and minerals in our foods, our tolerance for even a little stress is lowered to almost nil. Imagine missing all this nutrition from a child's diet and then sending the child to school to learn something. No energy except to compensate with hyperactive physical behavior caused by psychological stress, and we find not only that our children are disturbed but we ourselves begin to feel moody, uncertain and hooked on foods and snacks which give us a false sense of energy. The temporary boost we get from cheap carbohydrates such as sucrose and glucose used in soft drinks and junk foods will even enslave those who know better. Don't think it's all just ignorance. We often know the truth but we cannot help ourselves from grabbing the sweets even when we know they are harmful. We feel trapped in a prison of our own making. Here is an account of an intelligent woman who had a youthful attractive and active body and fell into a habit pattern:

> I gave up Cokes and all sweets entirely for seven
> years. I ate only healthy food, but I didn't feel that
> great. When I rediscovered sugar, my "low blood
> sugar" got better. After having gone headlong
> into health food and made myself sick, I tried to
> balance out with a mix of good and bad things.
> That seemed saner. But then when I left my
> husband, I wanted to do things I hadn't been
> doing. I especially got into Cokes. Often it seemed
> like ecstasy the feeling I had when drinking a
> Coke. Often it seemed like the only happiness
> I was able to control, since the other ones seemed
> to elude me. "At least there is always Coke,"
> I would say to myself. And I think, too, that it
> was a way of going back into childhood when I
> was happy or thought I was.
>   I find with sugar, as with alcohol, that the
> quantity is addictive. I can remember when one

martini before supper just didn't do it; I had to have two, but I don't handle liquor well at all, so I would be tipsy by suppertime. For me and most fat people, the meal doesn't feel finished til I have had a sweet. But then it gets to be that one cookie is not enough, and then two isn't enough and then three doesn't quite *do* it. The "finished" feeling does not come. But if I decide to cut down and I taper back down to one cookie then pretty soon, more seems *too* sweet. So there is a relativity of taste, and yet it seems like reality, i.e., it feels like three cookies really isn't enough, and yet you can't tell where the feeling is coming from or why it isn't enough. It just feels that way.

For myself, I like all the foods I had as a child and not many new ones. I like best the flowers that we were able to grow in New Mexico and not the ones that grow elsewhere. There is a kind of programming. I was into peanut butter in junior high but got over it. Then in San Diego, I was on Dr. Atkins diet, and one of the few things I could have that was any fun was two peanut butter crackers and some diet Dr. Pepper. So I got *hooked* on it! It began to seem like peanut butter was the most wonderful thing. And it got me back into Cokes a year later.

Some people think that the peanut butter is no good, but it isn't really that unhealthy, so I never can get motivated to change it. My slim friend says 'cook vegetables' and so I do, but then they are boring and take time and trouble and I feel it is better to be much happier with less bother, so I go back to my snacks. I could change if it seemed really better to me, but it never does.

Not all dieters will respond to this but they will quickly recognize the familiar psychological problem behind the physical urge to consume what you like, and see why you like what has been forbidden. The answer is, of course, that there is a certain happiness in getting what you want. This is very human and natural for people to react emotionally to those physical stimuli which give us a burst of quick energy and a nice taste on the tongue.

So how do we get control, willingly and without exercising tremendous effort? The answer is in balancing the needs for energy with something else which gives the same effect but does not give us the bad consequences. The energy drain feeling which makes us feel we are lacking some vital thing in life, can be conquered with Spirulina. Because Spirulina has a more efficient carbohydrate than sugar (rhamnose) and contains already made glycogen for immediate energy, a spoonful of Spirulina gives a burst of energy before our body goes on to digest and assimilate the 60–70% protein fraction of this amazing vegetable. Including the Spirulina three times a day with our free days as well as our diet days in Dr. Hills Slimming Plan gives us enough of the feeling of well-being to balance out the feeling of missing something. That feeling which acts on our appetite center can be controlled when we understand it and know what we can do about it. Within a short time of taking Spirulina and OB-1 vitamins we can feel the difference. This is why Spirulina is the central star piece, the shining light of the Dr. Hills Slimming Plan. But more than that, it is required to get rid of surplus energy piled up in fat. We must get our elimination system working and our insulin reactions more balanced with the galactomannan fiber. Then our craving for junk foods will disappear naturally because the chemicals in our blood will not give us the urge for sweetness. This urge is caused by insulin which wipes out the glucose, our energy source in the blood.

THE UNIQUE THING
ABOUT FIBER-LEAN ™

Fiber is the material surrounding the cell walls of plants. Fruits, vegetables and whole grains are all good sources of fiber, but we now eat half as much of these fiber-containing foods as our grandparents ate. To us it seems "normal" to eat a large proportion of processed foods from which the refining process has removed the fiber, but since the dietary fiber has been removed from our most commonly used foods, we are obliged to take it as a supplement. Yet most dietary fiber has little or no nutritional value. Most fiber products are indigestible and nutritionally worthless except for helping the bowel to eliminate. However, Dr. Hills discovered a new galactomannan fiber in Israel and noted the impressive nutritional qualities of this Israeli-researched product, which also contains nutritionally valuable arabinomannans which make it far superior to wheat bran in providing roughage to the diet. Therefore he is bringing all of its advantages to you in the Dr. Hills Slimming Plan.

Clinical studies at leading institutions in Israel have discovered that this special sugar-free extract, in addition to being a source of fibrous "bulk" with little starch, has a very unique nutritional effect. The following specifics of this nutritional fiber are expressed in mg. per 100 grams:

Inositol	60.0	Choline	30.0
Methionine	0.3	Niacin	1.0
Ascorbic Acid	3.0	Folic Acid	0.3
Biotin	0.02	Pyridoxine B-6	0.2
Riboflavin	0.1	Pantothenic Acid	0.1

This fiber has been researched at the Rambam Hospital and the Israel Institute of Technology Faculty of Medicine for its dietary effects on diabetes, and the discovery of its unique properites has caused considerable demand from the health specialists in Germany where this nutritional product is used with obese people.

Fiber Chart

These figures are based upon amounts of 3.5 ounces, in portions from which the inedible parts have been removed.

	CALORIES	FIBER (Grams)
ALMONDS		
Dried	598	2.6
Roasted and salted	627	2.6
APPLES		
Raw		
Not pared	58	1.0
Pared	54	.6
Cooked, with sugar	76	.5
APPLESAUCE, canned		
Unsweetened or artificially sweetened	41	.6
Sweetened	91	.5

	CALORIES	FIBER (Grams)
APRICOTS		
Raw	51	.6
Dehydrated, sulfured, nugget-type and pieces		
Uncooked	332	3.8
Dried, sulfured	260	3.0
Uncooked		
ARTICHOKES		
Cooked, boiled, drained	50	2.4
ASPARAGUS		
Raw spears	26	.7
Cooked spears, boiled, drained	20	.7
Canned spears		
Regular pack, drained solids	21	.8
Cooked, boiled, drained	22	.8
AVOCADOS, raw	167	1.6
BEANS, common, mature seeds, dry		
White, cooked	118	1.5
Red, cooked	118	1.5
Pinto, calico and red Mexican, raw	349	4.3
Other, including black, brown and Bayo, raw	339	4.4
BEANS, lima		
Cooked, boiled, drained	111	1.8
Canned, drained solids	96	1.8
BRAN		
Added sugar and malt extract	240	7.8
Added sugar and defatted wheat germ	238	6.5
BRAN FLAKES (40% bran), added thiamine	303	3.6
BRAN FLAKES with raisins, added thiamine	287	3.0
BRAZIL NUTS	654	3.1
BREADS		
Cracked wheat	263	.5
Raisin	262	.9
Rye		
American (⅓ rye, ⅔ flour)	243	.4
Pumpernickel	246	1.1
White	269	.2
Whole wheat	243	1.6
BROCCOLI		
Raw spears	32	1.5
Cooked spears, boiled, drained	26	1.5
Frozen	29	1.1
BRUSSELS SPROUTS		
Raw	45	1.6
Cooked, boiled, drained	36	1.6
Frozen	36	1.2

	CALORIES	FIBER (Grams)
BUCKWHEAT		
Whole grain	335	9.9
BREAD CRUMBS		
Dry, grated	392	.3
BREAD STUFFING MIX, dry form	371	.8
BREADFRUIT, raw	103	1.2
BULGUR (parboiled wheat)		
Dry, commercial, made from:		
Club wheat	359	1.7
Hard red winter wheat	354	1.7
White wheat	357	1.3
CABBAGE		
Raw	24	.8
Cooked, boiled until tender, drained	20	.8
Red, raw	31	1.0
Chinese	14	.6
CASHEW NUTS		
	561	1.4
CARROTS		
Raw	42	1.0
Cooked, boiled, drained	31	1.0
Canned	28	.6
CAULIFLOWER		
Raw	27	1.0
Cooked, boiled, drained	22	1.0
CELERY		
Raw	17	.6
Cooked, boiled, drained	14	.6
CHESTNUTS		
Fresh	194	1.1
Dried	377	2.5
CHEWING GUM	317	—
CHICKPEAS or garbanzos		
	360	5.0
COOKIES		
Assorted, packaged, commercial	480	.1
CORN PRODUCTS used mainly as ready-to-eat breakfast cereals:		
Corn flakes	386	.7
Corn, puffed	390	.4
Presweetened	379	.3
CRACKERS		
Cheese	479	.2
Graham	384	1.1
Soda	439	.2

	CALORIES	FIBER (Grams)
CRANBERRIES		
Raw	46	1.4
CRANBERRY SAUCE, sweetened, canned, strained	146	.2
EGGPLANT		
Raw	25	.9
Cooked, boiled, drained	19	.9
FIBER-LEAN	199	39
FLOUR		
Dark	333	1.6
Light	347	.5
LARD	902	—
LEEKS, bulb and lower leaf portion, raw	52	1.3
LENTILS		
Raw	340	3.9
Cooked	106	1.2
LETTUCE, raw	14	.5
MUFFINS	294	.1
OAT PRODUCTS used mainly as hot breakfast cereals:		
Cooked	62	.6
Oat and wheat cereal, cooked	65	.3
Oatmeal or rolled oats, cooked	55	.2
OLIVES, pickled, canned or bottled, ripe	129	1.4
ONIONS, raw	38	.6
ONIONS, young green (bunching varieties), raw		
Bulb and entire top	36	1.2
ORANGES		.5
PAPAYAS, raw	39	.9
PARSLEY, raw	44	1.5
PEAS AND CARROTS, frozen		
Cooked, boiled, drained	53	1.5
PECANS	129	1.4
PEPPERS, hot, chili		
Raw pods, excluding seeds	37	1.8
Canned:		
Pods, excluding seeds, solids and liquid	25	1.2
Chili sauce	20	1.0
PEACHES, raw	38	.6
PEANUTS		
Raw, with skins	564	2.4
Raw, without skins	568	1.9
POPCORN, popped		
Plain	386	2.2
Oiled and salt added	456	1.7
Sugar coated	383	1.1

	CALORIES	FIBER (Grams)
POTATOES		
Baked in skin	93	.6
Boiled in skin	76	.5
French fried	274	1.0
POTATO CHIPS	568	1.6
PRETZELS	390	.3
PRUNES		
Dehydrated, uncooked	344	2.2
Dried	255	1.6
PUMPKIN		
Raw	26	1.1
Canned	33	1.3
PEANUT BUTTER	581	1.9
PEARS		
Raw, including skin	61	1.4
PEAS, cooked, boiled, drained	43	1.2
PEAS, split, cooked	115	.4
RAISINS, natural (unbleached)		
Uncooked	289	.9
Cooked fruit and liquid, added sugar	213	.4
RASPBERRIES		
Raw	57	3.0
RHUBARB, raw	16	.7
RICE		
Brown, cooked	119	.3
White (polished), cooked	109	.1
Long-grain, cooked	106	.1
Precooked (instant), ready-to-serve	109	.1
ROLLS AND BUNS		
Danish pastry	422	.1
Plain (pan rolls)	298	.2
Sweet rolls	316	.2
Whole wheat rolls	257	1.6
RUTABAGAS		
Raw	46	1.1
Cooked, boiled, drained	35	1.1
RYE, whole grain	334	2.0
Rye wafers, whole-grain	344	2.2
SOYBEANS, cooked, boiled and drained	118	1.4
Miso	171	2.3
SOYBEAN CURD (tofu)	72	.1
SPINACH		
Raw	26	.6
Cooked	23	.6
STRAWBERRIES		
Raw	37	1.3

TOMATOES, ripe, raw	22	.5
WALNUTS, black	628	1.7
WHEAT PRODUCTS used as ready-to-eat breakfast cereals		
Wheat germ, toasted	391	1.7
Wheat puffed	363	2.0
Wheat shredded	354	2.3
WHEAT FLOURS		
Whole (from hard wheats)	333	2.3
All purpose or family flour, enriched	364	.3

TO HELP YOU STAY SLIM

Once you have succeeded in reaching your goal, the next goal will be to maintain the "new you" without slipping back. We are including a calorie chart to help you be aware that some foods more than others will help you stay slim. Some dieters like to stay ignorant of proteins, carbohydrates, fats, calories, or anything about foods that might upset their eating habits. They bury their heads in the sand like ostriches and eat four or five starches at one meal in blissful ignorance instead of balancing their nutrients. Or they eat a fast handful of peanuts in the belief that the amount (or the speed) is more important than the fact that peanuts are fats. These same dieters are also those who weigh every day and sadly wonder why the scales do not show any loss.

Awareness is essential to mastery, because you can't master what you cannot see. This is not to imply, however, that calories are the only factor that you must be aware of. It may be that at certain times you would choose a carbohydrate instead of a protein (for quicker energy) or you might even choose a tiny amount of fat, rather than either carbohydrate or protein, simply because fat is the slowest to digest and will last you longest (if for example, you are just running out of the house to be gone for four hours and you haven't time to eat). A protein digests slower than a carbohydrate but more

FOOD COMBINING FOR EASIER AND EFFICIENT DIGESTION

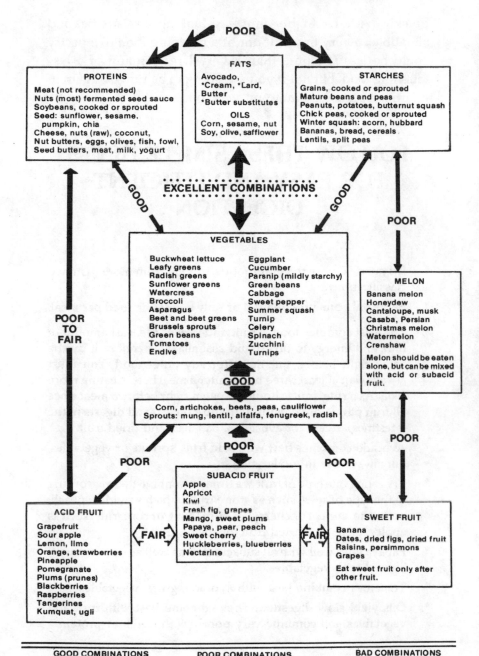

POOR

PROTEINS
Meat (not recommended)
Nuts (most) fermented seed sauce
Soybeans, cooked or sprouted
Seed: sunflower, sesame.
  pumpkin, chia
Cheese, nuts (raw), coconut,
Nut butters, eggs, olives, fish, fowl,
Seed butters, meat, milk, yogurt

FATS
Avocado,
*Cream, *Lard,
Butter
*Butter substitutes

OILS
Corn, sesame, nut
Soy, olive, safflower

STARCHES
Grains, cooked or sprouted
Mature beans and peas
Peanuts, potatoes, butternut squash
Chick peas, cooked or sprouted
Winter squash: acorn, hubbard
Bananas, bread, cereals
Lentils, split peas

GOOD

·······EXCELLENT COMBINATIONS·······

GOOD

POOR

VEGETABLES
Buckwheat lettuce
Leafy greens
Radish greens
Sunflower greens
Watercress
Broccoli
Asparagus
Beet and beet greens
Brussels sprouts
Green beans
Tomatoes
Endive

Eggplant
Cucumber
Parsnip (mildly starchy)
Green beans
Cabbage
Sweet pepper
Summer squash
Turnip
Celery
Spinach
Zucchini
Turnips

MELON
Banana melon
Honeydew
Cantaloupe, musk
Casaba, Persian
Christmas melon
Watermelon
Crenshaw

Melon should be eaten alone, but can be mixed with acid or subacid fruit.

POOR TO FAIR

GOOD

Corn, artichokes, beets, peas, cauliflower
Sprouts: mung, lentil, alfalfa, fenugreek, radish

POOR

POOR

POOR

POOR

SUBACID FRUIT
Apple
Apricot
Kiwi
Fresh fig, grapes
Mango, sweet plums
Papaya, pear, peach
Sweet cherry
Huckleberries, blueberries
Nectarine

ACID FRUIT
Grapefruit
Sour apple
Lemon, lime
Orange, strawberries
Pineapple
Pomegranate
Plums (prunes)
Blackberries
Raspberries
Tangerines
Kumquat, ugli

‹FAIR›

‹FAIR›

SWEET FRUIT
Banana
Dates, dried figs, dried fruit
Raisins, persimmons
Grapes

Eat sweet fruit only after other fruit.

GOOD COMBINATIONS	POOR COMBINATIONS	BAD COMBINATIONS
Protein and leafy greens	Protein and acid fruit	Protein and starch
Starch and vegetables	Leafy greens and acid fruit	Oil and starch
Oil and leafy greens	Leafy greens and subacid fruit	Fruit and starch
Oil and acid/subacid fruit		

quickly than a fat. In the same way, looking at relativities and situations, a very tiny amount of a fattening food like pastry could be less fattening than a very large amount of a less fattening food, but not if you are going to be hungry again in an hour because the amount was too tiny.

FOLLOW THESE SIMPLE HINTS FOR EASY AND EFFICIENT DIGESTION

* Do not mix more than four foods, or food from more than two classifications.

* Serve only one protein food or only one starch food per meal.

* The least complex food is fruit and it takes the least amount of time and energy to digest and assimilate. Therefore it can be eaten right before, but not after any other food. You must always wait at least three hours after a meal before eating more food. As a rule, fruits should be eaten right before a meal since all fruit passes directly through the stomach and digests in the intestines, except for avocados, bananas, and dried fruit.

* Avocado combines best with acid fruit, sprouts or vegetables, but always use in moderation.

* Try eating one type of fruit at a time or combine them according to the type of seed, such as stone fruit (which would be peach, nectarine, apricot or cherry) or citrus fruit, or core fruit (such as apples, pears), or dried fruit, or melon fruit.

* Papaya goes well with all subacid fruit as well as with bananas, but not with vegetables.

* Tomatoes combine best with avocado, green vegetables.

* Oils yield slow digestion. They combine best with fruit and vegetables and combine very poorly with starch or protein.

* All melons should be eaten alone in moderation. Too much can create gas.
* Healthy cell structure cannot be built through fermentation or putrefaction in the stomach or colon.
* Proteins combine best with salads or steamed vegetables to assure optimum digestion.
* Salads and steamed vegetables mixed with carbohydrates will also assure optimum digestion.
* Through proper food combining, the digestive system will be worked less, which will allow conservation of energy that the body can utilize for the cleansing of accumulated toxic waste.
* One of the main reasons for obesity is improper food combining, so study and use this food combining chart every day.
* Remember, the rule of the Dr. Hills Slimming Plan is three-quarters full, one-quarter for churning room.

Your digestive system requires different secretions to break down proteins, carbohydrates and fruits. When you poorly combine your food, such as when you eat a protein with a carbohydrate or starch, the different digestive juices when in contact with each other in the stomach will nullify each other's effectiveness. This will cause the protein to putrefy and the carbohydrates to ferment. The end result is gas and flatulence in the system.

CHART OF COMMON FOODS

Main List	Serving Size	Calories
Fish	1 slice (2"X2"X1" thick)	100
Canned fish packed in water	¼ cup	30
Tuna, salmon		
Oysters, shrimp	5 small	100
Clams	5 small	80
Crabmeat	3 oz.	80
Sardines	3 medium	90
Cheese, cheddar	1 slice (3½"X1½"X¼")	100

Cottage cheese	¼ cup	60
Egg (medium)	1	75
Natural cheeses:		
Roquefort	1 oz. (avoid if possible)	
		105
Swiss	1 oz. (avoid if possible)	105
Chicken	1 drumstick	90
	¼ breast	78
	thigh (medium)	95
Tofu (bean curd)	3½ oz.	72
Bouillon broth and consommé	1 cup	30
Chicken gumbo soup	1 cup	55
Chicken noodle soup	1 cup	50
Chicken with rice soup	1 cup	50
Clam or Manhattan chowder	1 cup	80
Cream of asparagus soup, with water	1 cup	65
Cream of chicken soup, with water	1 cup	95
Minestrone soup	1 cup (skim off fats)	105
Tomato soup, with water	1 cup	90
Vegetable soup	1 cup	80
Bouillon cube	1 cup	5
Olives, green	5 small or 3 large	15
Olives, ripe	3 small or 2 large	15
Dill pickles	1	15
Sweet pickles	1	20

Bread and Cereal List
(Please be sure to measure quantities carefully and do not exceed recommended amounts.)

Bread	1 slice	75
Cornbread	1½" cube	50
Muffin	1 (2" diameter)	134
Cooked cereal	½ cup	50
Dry cereal	¼ cup	25
Rice	½ cup, cooked	100
Spaghetti	½ cup, cooked	100
Egg noodles	½ cup, cooked	75
Graham crackers	2	50
Saltines	5	50
Oyster crackers	20	20
Soda crackers	3	40
Ry-Krisp crackers	2 triple crackers	50
Oatmeal, cooked	1 cup	130
Fiber-Lean	1 level tablespoon	22
Wheat, puffed	1 cup	55
Corn flakes (unsweetened)	½ cup	50
Ram Bam Bread	1 slice	70

Fats List

(Measure fats extremely carefully and avoid if possible.)

Butter	1 teaspoon	50
Margarine	1 teaspoon	30
Light cream	2 tablespoons	60
Heavy cream	1 tablespoon	50
Cream cheese	1 tablespoon	60
Salad dressing	1 tablespoon	60
Mayonnaise	1 teaspoon	50
Salad oil	1 teaspoon	30
Nuts	6 small	50

Fruit List*

(Fresh or canned or frozen fruits without added sugar or syrup only.)

Apple	1 small (2" diameter)	58
Applesauce	½ cup unsweetened	50
Apricots, fresh	2 medium	50
Apricots, dried	4 half apricots	100
Banana	½ small banana	50
Berries	1 cup	150
Blueberries	⅔ cup	85
Cantaloupe	¼ medium 6" diameter	85
Cherries	10 large	60
Dates	2	60
Figs, fresh	2 large	60
Figs, dried	1 small	30
Grapefruit	½ small	75
Grapes	12	75
Mango	½ small fruit	50
Orange	1 small	50
Papaya	⅓ medium fruit	70
Peach	1 medium	38
Apple juice	1 cup	120
Blackberries	1 cup	85
Cranberry juice cocktail	1 cup	170
Grapefruit juice	1 cup	90
(Unsweetened or fresh)		
Lemons	1	20
Lemon juice (fresh)	1 cup	60
Lime juice (fresh)	1 cup	65
Pineapple	1 cup	75
Plums	2	50
Raspberries (raw)	1 cup	70
Strawberries (fresh)	1 cup	55

Tangerines	2	80
Orange juice	1 cup	114
(frozen, diluted)		

Smoothie Ingredients:

Spirulina Powder	3 heaping teaspoons	80
Bee Sweet Pollen	1 tablespoon	39
Fiber-Lean	1 tablespoon	22
Lecithin^{Plus}	1 tablespoon	50
Manna Powder	½ ounce	55

Vegetable List

Pumpkin (canned)	1 cup	75
Tomato juice	1 cup	45
V-8 juice	1 cup	42
Carrot, raw	1 medium	30
Peas	½ cup	60
Corn	⅓ cup	50
Baked beans	¼ cup	80
Potato	1 (2" diameter)	85
Mashed potato	½ cup	100
Yams	¼ cup	50
Green beans, snap	1 cup	31

See Free List below

Milk List

Whole milk	1 cup	166
Evaporated milk	½ cup unsweetened	175
Powder milk	¼ cup without water	35
Buttermilk	1 cup	86
Skim milk	1 cup	87
Yogurt	1 cup	125

Free List

You may use cinnamon, garlic, lemon, mustard, mint, nutmeg, parsley, pepper, spices from Dr. Hills Spice Rack, vanilla and vinegar. Free foods include herb tea (without sugar or cream), fat-free broth, bouillon, unflavored gelatin, cranberries (prepared without sugar), rhubarb (prepared without sugar). The following vegetables have insignificant calories. Eat as much as you like raw or up to ONE cup cooked.

Asparagus	String beans	Peppers (green or red)
Broccoli	Tomatoes	Radishes
Brussels sprouts	Escarole	Sauerkraut
Cabbage	Salad greens	Squash, yellow summer
Celery	Leaf vegetables	Watercress
Chicory	Lettuce	Zucchini
Cucumbers	Mushrooms	Cauliflower
		Onion

CHANGING YOUR OWN HABITS

Since you and you alone are responsible for losing the weight you want to lose, you can set your own rules, depending on how self-disciplined you are. One of my students said to my secretary, Pam Osborn, some years ago, "It's easy for me not to eat sweet rolls, because I just don't buy them and then they're not around to tempt me." Pamela replied, "That doesn't work for me, because I just think they're right over there in the store and all I have to do is go get one!!" This is what I mean. What works for someone else won't necessarily work for you. And the diet books that tell you to chew your food more slowly or to eat your salad first, or never to read or watch TV while eating will only feel like coercion. So decide that you are going to tailor-make whatever rules you need, rather than be a sadist and make rules that you will rebel against in a few weeks' time. *Just find out what works for you.*

The pages that follow may trigger some ideas in your mind which will help you to reshape your own habit patterns. None of them is a must. The only must is that you must be neither too lenient with yourself nor too harsh, but treat yourself with loving discipline as you would treat a child by giving it full freedom to do whatever it chooses inside the broad limits of its own yard, so long as it does not go outside the gate. Children love this kind of discipline, even though they pretend to fight it, and the same is true of your own self, even though you may not be conscious of it. Each time you make a rule that you can actually follow and you stick to it every day, a subtle feeling of fulfillment will start to grow inside you.

When people challenge our habits we usually react, often with anger. Dieters get angry when someone points to their stomach protruding even slightly over the belt. This reaction is a tip-off, so if you find yourself doing it, you know that you are not only attached to the habit but also probably not working on it even though you may be telling yourself that you are reacting because you want to make your own rules and not be told by someone else. It is natural to fight for independence and self-rule over one's own body, and no one wants someone nagging them like their mothers used to nag them to drink their orange juice. To have someone telling you what to do or even hinting that you would be better off doing what they say creates a stubbornness, and unconsciously you will dig your heels in. But in order to lose weight, you have to be that "voice of discipline" yourself. Some diet books recommend tricking yourself by using smaller plates or by putting your sweets in the wrong cupboard when you want to diet. But the part of you that overeats is very cunning. It could get to its sweets even if you hid them under the house, and it will just laugh at any attempt to trick it. Somehow you will have to become the one who is doing the discipline, rather than the one who is resisting one's own good advice.

Tell people not to eat TV dinners, not to gobble food down fast, not to buy junk foods at the store, and the temptation to go to the store and buy those very things and gobble them down will come even stronger. Why is this? You have to understand that our habits are formed in the mind, not the body. The more people cannot get something because it is scarce, the more they want it. Drug habits are the same at the beginning; then later on, the body takes over and physically craves satisfaction. To understand the power of our minds over reality we have to change ourselves before we can change our habits. If we become dependent on anything, on anyone or on certain foods, we have to recognize that dependence is not self-mastery and it is in fact slavery. We know that we get angry about being enslaved and being told by others that we are out of self-control. So this frustration and anger must be used to get us into independence from sugar, from coffee or Coke or other habits which appear to become strong biological urges.

We don't listen to others when they tell us to lay off the cheese cake and ice cream. We just make a rationalization inside and do whatever we want to in secret if we can't do it openly. The ability to rationalize anything is the ability to deceive ourselves. The murderer can always rationalize why he had to kill someone. The terrorist or invader can always rationalize his actions in the killing of innocent populations. Dictators rationalize their need for power and, just as drug addicts rationalize all their actions, so do dieters create hundreds of reasons why they should eat and eat.

So it's no use appealing to reason and good sense. Some of the people with the problem are so intelligent they will always find a way to beat the authority and cheat. The Dr. Hills Slimming Program gives you three days to enjoy yourself and four days to balance so you don't feel cheated by not being able to cheat. What's the use of playing games with yourself if you are going to cheat on your diet plan? You may as well not fool yourself. So we do away with cheating by eating what you like on three days a week with only one rule—three-quarters stomach full!

Of course you are going to be tempted to cheat on three-quarters full if you say you are and if you believe you will. But if you do cheat, don't feel guilty. You will make up for it on your "shape up" day by living the law of balance, but your

dieting will be slower. In this way you will not feel deprived that you are forbidden, that there are things that rob you of the ability to make your own rules. You remain your own authority and you choose to *not* fool yourself four days a week.

The following lists are given in this spirit; you can choose them or not! If you choose them you get your birthright of a slimmer body about 50 percent quicker. But there is no hurry in Dr. Hills Slimming Program. You get there just the same even if like the tortoise you move slower. Make sure you are not like the hare who thought he could run fast and have a sleep on the way. Once you enter the race or play the game you will win only by staying on the plan long enough for it to work. When you reach the weight you want to be, you reward yourself with an extra "free day" so you lose weight to win. Losing to win is a principle not only in dieting but in the spiritual life too. You lose your attachment to life in order to find it, says Christ and his saints. That is a spiritual law. It is a law of the mind that the more you push, the harder it is to get a thought to go away. And it's the same in dieting. The more you resist, the more the temptations come back with force. Light Force makes things Light, and the Lighter you are with your mind and its power the easier your diet will become. You must let your thoughts of food go past; you don't fight them back or your will creates pressure. Meditate on your temptations before succumbing. You will find they will go away of their own accord it you let them go through you and out back of you. "Get thee behind me" is Christ's communication of this law of the mind. Not open confrontation, but an understanding of how the devil's power is only your resistance. Don't confront it head on; let the negative thought go right through and past you and it can't have anywhere to cling in your psyche. Try and bully it to go away and watch it come back not only next day but in the next five minutes. Haven't you noticed that people are obsessed with the negative?

These laws of the mind have been discovered by a long scientific research into the nature of evil and the nature of the spiritual life. They make the difference between your being a baddy or a goody, a self-righteous fanatic or a forgiving person when looking at others' weaknesses.

If you can look at your own weaknesses before you look at others' you will not only forgive others quicker but you will forgive yourself too. Forgiving yourself, however, cannot be done without doing something about the problem. If you keep repeating the pattern or habit after forgiving yourself for it, you will become spiritually and mentally stuck in a rut of your own making. You will try to get out of this rut by either preaching to others to change their lives and become fanatic, or you will go on an eating spree to cover up your feelings of inadequacy. You choose freely the self-righteous, all-knowing angry way, or you choose the humble way of forgiveness.

Forgive yourself and start again. As long as you keep trying and don't fool yourself you will eventually succeed. There is only yourself who can stop you from changing all your habits.

Make Your Own Rules

1. Think of eating as a separate experience, not to be confused or shared with other activities. Watching TV while eating makes you eat more food than you meant to eat and makes you taste and enjoy it less.
2. Don't eat fast, because satiety, the feeling of fullness, comes on slowly. Eating more slowly will give satiety a chance to catch up, and you will feel satisfied when three-quarters full.

3. Make a point of chewing your food. This will allow time for your blood sugar to rise and will allow smaller amounts of food to be more satisfying.
4. Eat the salad before the rest of the meal.
5. If you envy something someone else is eating, take one small bit of it so you won't feel you didn't get any, but if you cannot take one bite and leave the rest, then don't take the first bite.
6. Any time your stomach flashes a signal to your brain saying, "I'm hungry", be sure to ask yourself the question, "Am I really hungry?" It may be that you have just walked by a pastry shop or seen a picture of a candy bar in a magazine or seen a friend eating a cookie. So if the answer to this question is "no", eat Dr. Hills Galactomannan Nibblesticks.
7. Keep a bowl of already washed raw vegetables in your refrigerator and take it out when you feel the urge for a snack, or take some to work with you for your coffee breaks, so you are not tempted to get into junk foods. Also keep available tomato juice or sparkling mineral water which is delicious with a twist of lemon or lime.
8. If you have the urge to eat something sweet, you can satisfy it by a little-known technique: chew on a sour pickle. It will solve your problem in a matter of minutes.
9. Physical activity not only keeps your mind off high-calorie foods and snacks but it also helps metabolize the calories you've already consumed.
   a) Walk to your local grocery stores or shopping centers instead of driving.
   b) If you drive to work, try parking one or two blocks away from your place of employment. If you take a bus to work, get off one or two stops before your regular stop and walk the rest of the way. You can gradually extend this even further and you might even end up walking all the way.

c) If you take a lunch hour at your work, make use of the last fifteen or twenty minutes by taking a brisk walk. Breathe deeply and walk erectly and comfortably with your head held high. You may gradually build up the pace of your stride. The faster you walk, the more stored fuel you burn.

d) Try walking upstairs in office buildings rather than taking an elevator.

10. Don't buy problem foods and snacks in the first place. It won't hurt your family to take a break from junk foods either. If you don't have whipped cream and candy and pies and cake around the home, you won't be so tempted to eat them or to cheat.

11. Much overeating is a direct result of boredom. When you are feeling bored or frustrated you start to nibble on rich foods or snacks. If you discover this is the case, bring home books from the library. Join a dancing class or an aerobicize class or a bowling league. You might even take a class in a local school or college. Any activity or new interest will help keep your mind off food.

12. If you make homemade beef or chicken soup it is always wise to refrigerate the liquid first so you can remove the congealed fat before you eat the soup.

13. Try to eat your vegetables raw if possible. Use only fresh or frozen vegetables, not canned. And the same goes for fruit.

14. Shop from a prepared list and stick to it. Shop when you're NOT hungry.

CHAPTER 21

WHO IS DR. HILLS?
A Brief Sketch by His Wife
Who Has Known Him for Over Thirty Years

Who is this man with a greying beard and blue eyes that seem to penetrate into the heart of everything and everyone? Where does his seemingly inexhaustible energy and creativity come from? Is he an astute entrepreneur or is he a philosopher who has tuned into the eternal secret of how to blend the material, the scientific and the spiritual into one effective and potent manifestation? These are a few of the questions that people ask. The answer is that he is all of these and much more besides. He can turn his hand to anything. Christopher's inexhaustible energy and versatility can turn in a flash and apply itself with the same concentration to writing a book as to landscaping a garden. The same meticulous care goes into the lighting of a campfire and the developing of a new product for the Light Force Company.

What are his motives? What drives this man to use every ounce of energy to achieve his goal? What is that goal? Deep concern and love for humanity is the motive force behind all his work, and it was this concern that set him out on a mission of research into nutritional algae, a food that needed only sunlight and water to make it grow. Over twenty-five years ago, he and his Japanese friend and colleague, Dr. Hiroshi Nakamura, joined forces to perfect a strain of edible algae that was more digestible than the Chlorella already being consumed in large quantities in Japan. They explored Spirulina, the algae with the little spiral cells.

Hiroshi Nakamura

Neither of the two men was wealthy, so they tried to interest businessmen and governments in financing Spirulina growing projects in various parts of the world, preferably in the continents where malnutrition and starvation were most severe. Presidents and government officials paid lip service to their vision and gave lukewarm encouragement to their projects and proposals. Some saw in the enterprise a chance to play politics, and others saw an opportunity to make money. In the end, frustrated by bureaucrats and self-seeking businessmen, Christopher turned away from them all and founded the Light Force Spirulina Company in 1979.

The first
Light Force
facility in
Boulder
Creek, CA.

His goal was not only to supply the health-conscious society of the United States with a nutritious product but to use that same society to gain support and credibility for his vision of solving the hunger problem. If Spirulina became acceptable in America and was seen to improve health, then the proceeds of the sales of Spirulina could finance more production that would eventually bring down the price of Spirulina and put it within the reach of more and more people.

What actually happened, in July 1981, was that Spirulina became famous overnight, and then the businessmen all jumped on the bandwagon and greedily grabbed whatever Spirulina they could get, diluted it and passed it off on the public as "100% pure". Greed got the better of the Mexican suppliers too, and they ignored their contract with Dr. Hills and supplied the new customers at an inflated price, thus encouraging people who were not health-conscious but money-conscious and were out to make a profit at the expense of the public.

There was no alternative now but to grow Spirulina himself, so Christopher set up his own research laboratories in the United States, Kenya, Israel and other countries and got

This micro-scopic view of Spirulina shows its spiral nature.

ready not only to produce a totally pure strain of the nutritious food but also to discover less expensive growing methods that could eventually be taught to people in the underdeveloped countries.

The solving of the hunger problem was still his guiding star, but he is no starry-eyed idealist. He understands how humans think and work and how their selfishness and self-interest can thwart their higher purpose. There are two mainstreams to his work. He personally supervises the research into every new nutritional product, working side by side with his managers in the marketing and product development for the Light Force Company. At the same time, he explores every possibility for growing Spirulina in America.

His main work, however, without which he feels the work for better nutrition would be useless, is concerned with the whole person—body, mind and spirit. Those who work with him have come to recognize the truth of his words that echo like a refrain through all his speaking and writing: "You cannot change the world until you change yourself." Not everyone who hears those words really understands what he is saying. When he was a young businessman in the West Indies, he did not understand them himself. In those early days, his philosophy was very much like that of many young entrepreneurs: "First I'll make a million dollars and then people will take some notice of me and I'll use the money to do some good in the world". Before we were married, we would spend many hours discussing this decision and I would quote the scripture, "Seek ye first the kingdom of Heaven and all these things shall be added unto you". By the age of thirty he *was* a millionaire, but the urge to retire from his World Spice Company and other international businesses was getting stronger and stronger, and his keen concentration on business deals in spices and other commodities was getting less and less. When he became a victim of a slump in pimento and ginger on the world markets, he took it as a signal to leave the world of trading. Gradually he closed down his ten businesses or put in managers or sold the companies to his employees. He did not return to any large-scale business project until 1979, when he founded the Light Force Spirulina Company. Between 1956 and 1980, he researched the nature of consciousness, explored all the great teachings of the world and travelled through Europe, the Middle East and Asia in search of others who also knew that man's true destiny and fulfillment lay not in making money or in gaining power or in preaching to others, but in selflessness and self-conquest or mastery over the selfish ego and all its deceptive tricks.

When he founded the Light Force Company, he did not wait until he had a million dollars to back him. He had realized that if he put the needs of others first, the necessary financial resources would come automatically, because the work would be in tune with the law of the cosmos. And this has proved to be true.

Thousands of people in many countries know Christopher Hills from his books and his work to solve the world hunger problem. Very few of them have had the opportunity to discover what kind of a man he is in daily life. When people eventually meet him or come to work for his companies, they discover not only the tremendous resourcefulness which constantly inspires and motivates whatever he does, but also the wide range of his personality which responds like a mirror to those he encounters. The proud and self-opinionated find him arrogant; the humble and sincere are moved by his gentleness and understanding. His uncompromising ruthlessness in getting to the truth makes him feared by hypocrites and bigots and others who try to "get away with something" or to compromise with mediocrity. His deep understanding of human nature penetrates all masks and phoniness, but those who are open and spontaneously outspoken, like children, love to be with him, to laugh at his jokes and to share in the warmth of his love.